EMORY UNIVERSITY STUDIES IN LAW AND RELIGION

John Witte Jr., General Editor

BOOKS IN THE SERIES

Power over the Body, Equality in the Family:
Rights and Domestic Relations in Medieval Canon Law
Charles J. Reid Jr.

Religious Liberty in Western Thought
Noel B. Reynolds and W. Cole Durham Jr., eds.

Political Order and the Plural Structure of Society
James W. Skillen and Rockne M. McCarthy, eds.

The Idea of Natural Rights:
Studies on Natural Rights, Natural Law, and Church Law, 1150-1625
Brian Tierney

The Fabric of Hope: An Essay
Glenn Tinder

Liberty: Rethinking an Imperiled Ideal
Glenn Tinder

Religious Human Rights in Global Perspective: Legal Perspectives
Johan D. van der Vyver and John Witte Jr., eds.

Natural Law and the Two Kingdoms:
A Study in the Development of Reformed Social Thought
David VanDrunen

Early New England: A Covenanted Society
David A. Weir

God's Joust, God's Justice: Law and Religion in the Western Tradition
John Witte Jr.

Religious Human Rights in Global Perspective: Religious Perspectives
John Witte Jr. and Johan D. van der Vyver, eds.

BUILDING CULTURES
OF TRUST

Martin E. Marty

A Project of the Trust Institute
State University of New York at Stony Brook

WILLIAM B. EERDMANS PUBLISHING COMPANY
GRAND RAPIDS, MICHIGAN / CAMBRIDGE, U.K.

Published 2010 by

Wm. B. Eerdmans Publishing Co.

2140 Oak Industrial Drive N.E., Grand Rapids, Michigan 49505 /

P.O. Box 163, Cambridge CB3 9PU U.K.

Printed in the United States of America

14 13 12 11 10   7 6 5 4 3 2 1

Library of Congress Cataloging-in-Publication Data

Marty, Martin E., 1928-

Building cultures of trust / Martin E. Marty.

p.   cm.   — (Emory University studies in law and religion)

ISBN 978-0-8028-6546-5 (pbk.: alk. paper)

1. Trust.   2. Religion and science.

3. Trust — Religious aspects — Christianity.   I. Title.

BJ1500.T78M37   2010

261.5'5 — dc22

2009048009

www.eerdmans.com

We have . . . defined culture as 'regularities in the behaviour, internal and external, of the members of a society, excluding those regularities which are clearly hereditary in origin.' 'Culture' here is a general or mass-noun; it points to a class of elements in our experience, just as 'milk' and 'wheat' and 'mankind' do. How then shall we define the singular noun, 'a culture' or 'the culture', as used in such expressions as 'the culture of the Eskimos' . . . 'a primitive culture', and so on?

We might . . . define a culture as a distinctive assemblage of culture-traits and complexes regularly found together. . . .

Often the term is used of segments of a society, classes, professions and age-groups; we speak of 'middle-class culture' or 'adolescent culture'. . . . [It] is as segments of larger societies that we usually think of them.

PHILIP BAGBY

Contents

Acknowledgments

———◦◉◦———

Robert P. Crease, chair of the philosophy department at Stony Brook University, with the help of his colleagues and staff, served as host for my time in the Trust Institute at the university as both seminar leader and speaker for the Provost's Lecture Series in 2008. I thank Professor Crease and the hosts of the Templeton Research Lecture Series for the hospitality, encouragement, and intellectual stimulus. Among the numerous faculty members with whom I consulted or conversed while there, most helpful were Fred Goldhaber, professor in the C. N. Yang Institute for Theoretical Physics and the university's philosophy department, along with Stephen Spector, professor and chairman of the department of English. I also want to acknowledge the stimulus and substantive comments of John Witte Jr., director of the Center for the Study of Law and Religion at Emory University. Reinder Van Til, editor at Wm. B. Eerdmans Publishing Company, made major editorial contributions, for which I am grateful, just as I thank Harriet J. Marty for her customary and exemplary role as "in-house" critic and editor.

CHAPTER 1

To Build Cultures of Trust

⸻ ⊷◉⊶ ⸻

C onversations during the seasons in which this book was in process often went something like this:

"So you are writing a book on 'trust.' I don't associate you with that topic. Why did you take it up?"

My answer: "There *has* been some modest association. I have edited two little books with the word 'trust' in the title — they were written for specialized audiences — but now I hope you will associate me with the theme. This time it has a broader base and is aimed at a general readership."

The conversation partner: "Again, why did you take it up? You must think that trust is an urgent issue."

"Yes."

"If it's urgent," the partner would say, "why doesn't it show up in the opinion polls where citizens rank issues in their order of importance?"

"This is not the kind of topic that pollsters can easily address," I say. "It's harder to frame questions about 'trust' — or 'faith' or 'hope' or 'love' — than it is to ask for opinions about definite, hard-edged choices, such as, 'Do you favor bombing a nation that might become a nuclear threat?' 'Do you favor this party or that presidential candidate?' Trust is a more elusive theme."

The conversation partner typically continues with something like this: "Then how do you determine that this topic deserves so much attention?"

"Begin by looking in the mirror and observing yourself," I say. "You take pains to ward off identity theft because you don't trust the crooks out there. You are wary of potential scam artists who lead you to mistrust much of what is offered on your computer screen. You have a friend whose marriage broke up because a once-trusted spouse broke a covenant. You are careful about writing recommendations or endorsements because you ask yourself, 'Do I trust this person enough to risk my reputation on commending her character and potential performance?' Here is one that is often overlooked: Do you trust experts — for example, scientists — who have so much control of your life? Or, for one more sample: Do you trust the clergy, once presumably subjects of simple trust, when so many make headlines by betraying trust?"

After such an exchange, I would get something like this volley back from friends who are ready to become critical readers:

"So, what do you think you can do about the threats to trust or the breakdown of trust? No one elected you to the office of Improving Trust Relations or to anything else. The world is not waiting for self-appointed experts to rescue them from those who cause people to mistrust or distrust other people or institutions. Does being a historian give you a special vantage point, a set of tools, any kind of expertise that you might put to work to address the theme?"

"I am not sure I would trust anyone," I reply, "who makes very big claims about his expertise on the subject of trust. I am sure that historians can at best make small claims, contributing their part by the stories they choose, the ways they tell them, and the kinds of analysis that go with their work."

"Stop! I'm busy," my presumed conversational partner responds. "Make your case that historians have any special angle on such a topic as this."

"Well, think about it. What do historians write about that does not very directly or at least implicitly come down to 'trust'? War, diplomacy, treaty-making and treaty-keeping, the making of laws and policies, the operations of churches and other voluntary associations. Or, closer to home in what is called 'social history,' marrying and divorcing and child-rearing are finally about overcoming mistrust and distrust or demonstrating trustworthiness. The historian who writes stories about these does not have to be a scold or a police officer, a policymaker or a know-it-all. But he or she can encourage the development of curiosity, take notes, do research, reflect, and then emphasize the issue of trust in human history and present-day affairs. Page through newspapers, if you can still locate some, or consult the Internet, and you will find in any given day's headlines and stories accounts of events that historians tomorrow and ever after can see related to trust. They do not have to reduce everything to that subject. Nor do they need to make extravagant claims for their treatment of it, or of their potential for making some contribution in the areas they have chosen and defined."

The historian — or at least this historian — next hears from the other: "So, let me ask what is *your* shtick, your special angle, your preliminary discovery or proposal, your potential contribution?"

This historian replies: "My shtick, my angle, is this: First, any talk of improving trust must begin with the individual, her character, her resolve, her potential for change. We have to start there, though my approach has a more or less social drive, one that builds on individual commitment. Since plenty of writers through the ages have discussed personal trust, I will treat it mainly in the beginning of the book before turning over to others the development of the theme. Some of them address the questions about the individual as part of their lifelong research and writing."

"So, if the individual in isolation is only a part of the trust equation," says our unsatisfied, still-curious invented interlocutor, "I suppose you are going to turn cosmic on us and offer a generic and universal address to the issue of trust. I suppose you have a plan for making the institutions of advertising, televising, educating, war-making, caregiving, and so on better carriers of trust relations."

Now the historian says, "Stop! There are many steps along the way between the isolated, self-reforming individual at one extreme, and at the other extreme, the custodians of large establishments and institutions that do not appear to be very malleable and are not prospects for massive, immediate, and permanent change."

"Such as?"

"Such as what this book is about. It relates the individual to social forms, called 'cultures' and 'subcultures,' that can be open to change and can be changed. You can call this approach 'meliorative,' as I do, because it advocates understandings and strategies that can improve ('make better') the conditions of trusting. It is not 'meliorist,' which would imply an ideological commitment to the belief that things *will* get better. I call that approach unrealistic and utopian, which this book is not.

"In this project I envision ways in which trust can become more evident and can help and enrich social pockets of people and institutions. I am referring to people coming together, exerting ever-increasing influence on each other and on other gatherings and subcultures. You can call this approach 'incremental,' as I do, which implies improvement by degrees.

"To illustrate: rather than becoming frustrated when no inclusive and expansive policy or proposal is likely to be found, followed, and realized, those who have contributed to the growth of incremental subcultures or cultures of trust can begin to realize values associated with their growth. Finding employment at a workplace where being trustworthy is traditional and standard has an immediate payoff. Where trust prevails, policing is less necessary, so trust is economical. Being part of an institution of higher learning where honor codes are honored — a student would not think of violating them — means that potential cheating by others does not mean a comparative loss of one's record of achievements. Seeing trust restored in congregations or denominations where there has been a crisis of trust — usually over sexual matters, but sometimes financial or theological matters — contributes to a spiritually rich and vocationally rewarding outcome.

"In what will become a virtual case study, I want to concentrate on problems of trust in discourse, in human communication, using the example of discourse among and between scientists and religious thinkers, remaining aware, of course, that many people are both scientists and religious people. Of course, the case study would not resolve conflicts that may and do occur on the science-and-religion front. However, analyzing them can help make possible the beginnings of helpful conversations across the boundaries of the scientific and religious vocations and professions. Such conversations fit the 'ameliorative' and 'incremental' intentions of this book, which I conceive of as a modest contribution but also, I hope, a hopeful sign."

At about this point, my dialogue partner would interrupt what has now become a monologue:

"The book is about discourse that has to do with science, religion, and public life. Where do I come in? I am not a scientist, not particularly involved with religion, and I think that public life gets along all right as long as leaders in various fields are not fighting. As for the concept and practice of 'discourse,' I don't get invited to conferences or forums where high-level people discourse, or even converse, about weighty matters. I think I am a good enough citizen and have broad interests, but I still have to ask: How does any of this involve me and my kind?"

"Thanks for bringing to the fore the question of audience or readership," I respond. "I could begin by reminding you, my conversation partner, that all of us are affected daily by what scientists say and do, and the meaning of what they do affects everyone who eats, sleeps, goes to the doctor or pharmacist, or has a sense of wonder about the universe as a whole or in close-up. Next, the vast majority of Americans are at least to some degree involved with religion, including its institutions, in both positive and negative ways. When religious leaders overstep — and overstepping seems to be the main business of some religious leaders these years — we suffer in politics and social relationships. More than that, most of us, at least at times, experience doubt, disappointment, and the edge of despair; or, conversely, we can get ecstatic about things of the spirit. If we are thrown off our quests by challenges unmet, we suffer. As for public life, which includes so much more than just politics, issues of our two realms — science and religion — meet in the arena of that life. And science and religion have company in commerce, entertainment, the arts, education, and more. An open flow of communication, whether critical or affirmative, is vital to the development of trust as part of the goal of building cultures in a complex society."

Specifics, Hard News, and Relevant Examples

While imagining that conversation, I often wanted to interrupt the plot to provide specifics. Contending that some things are relevant because they illustrate broken trust is one thing; pointing to or calling to mind instances is another. They must be of a kind that the reader can connect with because they are so important, so vivid, so memorable, so threatening even in their afterlife.

I am going to provide a baker's dozen of examples, inviting readers to use their recall of each of them to prompt remembrance of others. For the moment, I will make no effort to arrange them in category-tight compartments, but intentionally keep in mind something of the random character with which such evidences reach us. These are samples from the most recent years of this new millennium, presenting themselves to anyone using the television remote control to scan the day's news, or to read the headlines in the newspapers and news weeklies. They figuratively scream, "This is relevant! Deal with it!"

9/11 and Conspiratorial Thinking

The millennium opened with a challenge to American security occasioned by the successful destruction of the World Trade Center, enormous damage to the Pentagon, and the annihilation of 3,000 lives. These 9/11 events made it impossible for citizens mentally to reconstruct a remembered image of security from before September 11, 2001. The traumatic event inspired inquiries that gave reasons to mistrust national security agencies, military defense, even the ability for the nation to defend itself. So shattering and nearly incomprehensible was it that, in the minds of millions and the writing of not a few, it became the classic occasion for expressing mistrust: indulging in conspiracy theories.

The Economic Crisis

Only six or seven years after 9/11, trusting Americans were jolted again, this time by a downturn in many portions of the economy and threats to the whole economy itself. The coming of the crisis, in its many expressions and citizens' interpretations of those expressions, evoked and displayed a range of suspicion, mistrust, and angry attacks that left everyone — the careful planners as well as those who had not kept their guard up — wary about investing confidence in the markets, the larger economy, the national complex, and the world economy. Some of the suspicion and anger was directed at banking and its kin centers of power.

Banks and Lenders

Americans in general believed that financial institutions were so apparently efficient that it was possible — across the economic spectrum — to borrow and lend and to risk, with good hope of gain. In the midst of the crisis, banks were exposed to failure, and many did fail. Trust in "the free-enterprise market economy," which had been virtually un-

6

challenged years earlier, now all but disappeared on many fronts. For example, banks and investment firms, which had acquired reputations for being secure and most of whose funds were guaranteed to be protected, adopted policies of such high risk that they were doomed to failure and were beyond rescue. The guarantees meant little now, which led millions to lose faith in banks in general.

Mistrust of Government as a Rescue Agency

Most — but by no means all — Americans were convinced that the failure of these institutions could bring down the whole economy. Even as they continued to mistrust inefficient government regulatory agencies, they recognized that on some terms or other, government agencies had to "step in" and "bail out" banks and other companies considered "too big to fail." People found enough short-sightedness, incompetence, and corruption to occasion a new mistrust of "big government" at a time when government was forced to be active.

From Mortgage-Lending to Foreclosures

What, it may fairly be asked, was at the heart of the expansion in home ownership or the high-risk borrowing for housing in which the borrower never intended to live? It was a set of practices, it may confidently be answered, that depended on trust, a trust that was routinely broken. At one end were subprime mortgages that were often deceptively presented by the lender via adjustable-rate mortgages; they were often sold on misleading terms by means of high-range investing connected with financial firms whose practices were characterized as relatively safe but whose value inevitably crashed like a house of cards.

Retirement Accounts

Many people — if not most — who were planning retirement or had retired tended to be careful and trusting, since it was their own "evening of life" resources on which they had to count. They worked with trusted financial consultants and investors. After the sudden loss of large percentages of such nest eggs, would insecure citizens so readily trust their counselors or the custodians of their fortunes? They risked, often conservatively, and lost their security — usually through little fault of their own,

Criminal Economic Activity

If early in the new millennium the name Enron and officers of the company holding that name became the designation for a classic case of criminal deception, years later Bernard Madoff was the memorable name that represented total betrayal of trust, which in turn amounted to the loss of billions among trusting investors. Between Enron and Madoff there were virtually daily accounts of criminal trust-breaking activity.

Bribery and Influence-Peddling

I am writing these lines in the state of Illinois, where governors and other high state and city officials have not infrequently ended their careers in jail — or should have — after they were exposed for bribery, corruption, and the general cheating of their fellow citizens. They have found company in many other states of the union and among commercial interests everywhere. They may not have been "worse" than their predecessors (trust-breaking is a long-practiced tradition in this state), but the size and scope of the shady and overtly criminal activity in an age when media can readily bring it to the public eye has spread the awareness that there are reasons to mistrust leaders of government as well as those of private companies.

Media Deception

This is more difficult to attend to in polarized America, where those at one pole can show how untrustworthy are the media that cater to "the other side," and vice versa. Yet an age of media dominance as a form of communication has produced new challenges to trust-making. Sometimes it has taken the form of grossly deceptive advertising; at other times it appears as distorted and lying communication — but constitutionally protected withal. Who can trust "the media" as they are portrayed by other media who do not consider themselves "mainstream" but are often masters of deception themselves? What can one trust on television or radio or — in the decade of new development — personal blogging and subversive message-sending that is subject to no agreed-on canon of truth-telling.

Religious Institutions Breaking Trust

As more and more religious institutions have adopted unmonitored means of marketing, financial scandals among many enterprises, often megachurches, have led to mistrust of church and synagogue. The scandal known by the code words "priestly abuse" has rocked Catholicism. Sometimes the aggrieved were adults who heard stories that led them to no longer trust their children to priests, whom they now perceived as predators; sometimes they were communicants-at-large reacting to stories of bishops who protected pedophiles and had to pay out billions of dollars to victims. Anyone who reported on celibate Catholic priests who had broken trust was soon called on to note that Protestant and other religious leaders had broken trust with their spouses through adulteries, leaving congregations staggered.

Mistrust of the Religious "Stranger"

Usually the Muslim is seen to be the suspicious stranger who might be a terrorist or a supporter of terrorists. America has long reckoned with religious diversity and has come to terms with "the other" — sometimes imaginatively and sometimes reluctantly. In the new millennium, the imaginative view of religious diversity still serves the public well, and some accommodating yet reluctant kinds of people have gone along to keep civil peace. But there are others who portray Muslims, or whoever represents "the other" to various groups, as threats to the republic.

The Exploited and Exploitable Public

In this book I will be regarding citizens and believers, "the public," as having capabilities for making judgments about trust-breakers and instruments for improving trust. But publics are no more naturally, persistently, and assuredly wise and fair than are the individuals who make them up. And the public can be manipulated and exploited to the point that they break bounds of civility and stimulate mistrust. When a member of Congress breaks all rules of decorum of such a setting as one did when he shouted "You lie!" to the president as he spoke formally, he was trying to stimulate mistrust. The same is true of those segments of the public who were aroused to shout disruptively at the so-called town-hall meetings. I would be mistrusted by my readers if I left the impression that only one party, one set of populist crowds, or one ideological group of television viewers were exploitable or setting out to exploit publics in confusing times. One can adduce plenty of examples across the spectrum to point to the risks to the nation if people cannot hear each other in matters of legitimate controversial encounters.

A Problem among the Professions

This is one of the longest-recognized forces among mistrusters, one that is enhanced now as the professions become more competitive and specialized. Among the many examples that exist, I will mention one here that I will elaborate on in later chapters. The stakes have never been higher than they are now in realms where "science" and "religion" are shorthand terms for large minorities in various professions who have been mistrustful of each other. This is evident to anyone who reads the polls, which find religious people suspicious of scientists on many fronts — those professionals they see as threatening to their faith and their future. The polls reveal that significant minorities — or even majorities — among the citizens, often on religious grounds, mistrust specialists in evolutionary thinking.

Turning that suspicion around, many among the scientists, well aware that religious leaders and their flocks have often blocked scientific inquiry, carry that awareness over into contemporary life, where new scientific research is desperately urgent and necessarily controversial. Hence they are reluctant to trust any scientists who are religious and who give voice to their religious commitments — even in proper contexts. In these postmodern and "post-Enlightenment" times, when a particular form of skeptical reason no longer has unquestioned hegemony, there are fewer reasons for people in the religious and scientific professions to fail to hear the other or consider the possibility of working together for the human good.

Most often when there are conflicts (below the level of politics) among scientists vis-à-vis "religionists," many on each side lack a conceptual or linguistic framework for understanding what the other does. Later in the book I will diagnose this misunderstanding as what the philosophers call a "category mistake." If this fallacy is properly recognized and addressed, it can be erased and a fresh basis for common understanding and trust can emerge. For now, though, we will list this as a zone of mistrust in a world where so much depends on what happens in the "worlds" of science and religion.

In all these cases we have seen that expressions of mistrust and violations of trust are not merely individually specific but belong to cultures, or at least subcultures, some of them marked by professions and institutions. Whoever seeks to contribute to the restoration of trust will necessarily have to work toward the building of cultures of trust.

"Building" and "Building Cultures" as a Goal

We now go on to investigate why the *building* of cultures is appropriate in this work of analysis and advocacy. Cultures by nature are so diverse, their shapes so protean, their boundaries ordinarily so fluid, that they look too elusive to be associated with any act of building. Ordinarily, we think simply of constructing buildings, which are singular, their shapes defined by architects and builders. To contend that "building cultures" is an appropriate concept necessitates defining what building or constructing can mean here.

The first dictionary definition is graphic but obvious when it refers to "constructing or erecting a building." It is the fourth definition, marked *fig.* (for "figurative") that applies here: "to construct, frame, raise, by gradual means (anything that is compared to an edifice, as a philosophical system, a literary work, a reputation, an empire)." The word "gradual" indicates that such building is the result of a process, not a product of a kind that someone merely unpacks in order to connect it immediately with specific issues or incidents.

That part was comparatively easy. Defining a culture, however, remains a venture that provides work for numberless lexicographers and essayists, few of whom may expect to come to agreement with each other. For thirty-five years, one-third of my own professorial assignment was to teach the humanities in a curricular slot named "The Committee on the History of Culture." We faculty and students tirelessly debated what such a quasi-discipline could include. Now, in these postmodern times and during my postretirement years, the humanities division of our university — evidently having given up on the task of finding its focus and setting its boundaries — has quietly abandoned the academic-style committee. Yet, though the curricular name has disappeared, the concept of culture certainly has not. It survives to serve its own protean and viscous purposes.

Fortunately, scholars can proceed on projects like this without settling on a single and simple definition of culture. But they would have plenty of choices, should they wish to do so. In a pioneering work, anthropologists A. L. Kroeber and Clyde Kluckhohn present and analyze 161 definitions of culture.[1] But they spend little time on our subject, preceded as it is by an indefinite article: *a* culture.

Philip Bagby took a run at defining it in his *Culture and History: Prolegomena to the Comparative Study of Civilizations.* During our campus discussions I never found a more appropriate and succinct summary than his. It serves as the epigraph to this book:

> We have . . . defined culture as 'regularities in the behaviour, internal and external, of the members of a society, excluding those regularities which are clearly hereditary in origin.' 'Culture' here is a general or mass-noun; it points to a class of elements in our experience, just as 'milk' and 'wheat' and 'mankind' do. How then shall we define the singular noun, 'a culture' or 'the culture', as used in such expressions as 'the culture of the Eskimos' . . . 'a primitive culture', and so on?
>
> We might . . . define a culture as a distinctive assemblage of culture-traits and complexes regularly found together. . . .
>
> Often the term is used of segments of a society, classes, professions and age-groups; we speak of 'middle-class culture' or 'adolescent culture'. . . . [It] is as segments of larger societies that we usually think of them.[2]

1. A. L. Kroeber and Clyde Kluckhohn, *Culture: A Critical Review of Concepts and Definitions* (New York: Vintage, 1963).

2. Philip Bagby, *Culture and History: Prolegomena to the Comparative Study of Civilizations* (Berkeley: University of California Press, 1958), p. 93.

Earlier in his book, while discussing "culture" as such, Bagby lists some major elements that anthropologists study. These include "the major departments of human activity: religion, politics, economics, art, science, technology, education, language, customs and so on." For such specialists, approaching "culture" meant also examining the realities behind such words. As Bagby puts it, these are "modes of behaviour, ways in which human beings act. They worship gods, struggle for political power, buy and sell goods, paint pictures and so on; activities all of which may be described as culture." Bagby then adds to this list "ideas, knowledge, beliefs, norms, values and other things, which would not normally be described as behaviour." He emphasizes the two areas to which we will give most attention when he discusses some crucial approaches to trust in the two fields that I will italicize here: "*Religion,* for instance," he says, "includes religious beliefs and religious experience as well as religious practices, while *science* covers a body of knowledge as well as the activities involved in acquiring that knowledge."[3]

Later, when discussing religion and science in connection with each other, I am going to make much of the modes through which they are experienced and to which they give particular voices. Bagby also mentions this as he continues: "In part, at least, these non-behavioural kinds of culture can be described as *modes* of thinking and feeling; they are features of that inner 'mental' activity which we can observe only in ourselves and must presume to exist in others. *Modes of thinking and feeling,* then, as well as *modes of behaviour* in the narrow sense, are among the objects included in the class of objects we call 'culture.'"[4]

Any of the cultures Bagby mentions — and we could add more, such as cultures of Buddhist monks, motorcycle gang members, or university sororities — is of potential interest here if and insofar as elements of trust accompany them; they do this in most if not all human social expressions. Thus some sorority members trustworthily adhere to honor codes because their congenial and chosen subculture cultivates such codes and honor, while others may not. The same may be said of some members of motorcycle gangs or monks.

Since I will be making much of subcultures on which individuals, small groups, and movements can gain influence, it will be helpful to cite Bagby, whose definitions of culture are dominant in this book, to

3. Bagby, *Culture and History,* p. 77.
4. Bagby, *Culture and History,* p. 77 (emphasis added).

13

see how he deals with subcultures. Rather than define them, he points to behavioral regularities:

> When we come to delimit the society or segment of a society which defines a sub-culture, the actual individuals to be included may often turn out to be defined by common elements in their behaviour, that is by the distinctive features of their sub-culture. Thus the middle-class or the professional group of clergymen are known by their behaviour, by what they do. . . . [T]he cultural differences are often clearer than the geographical boundaries.[5]

Thus the segment of a society that is distinctive because its participants embody, exemplify, justify, and expect expressions of trust is a subculture more definitely than is the group of citizens living in the Third Ward or in a valley. One professional association of educators or bankers that has cultivated expressions of trust will differ from another association of people in a similar profession, associations in which people wink at payments under the table and expect illegal payoffs.

We can lift out and examine some elements that Bagby notes as they might appear in cultures of trust and apply them to subcultural definition. Therefore, we will look for "regularities in . . . behaviour." If a person takes a consistent part in such a company of volunteers, it does not surprise us when we observe him and his co-volunteers keeping trust with the poor whom they serve and with his colleagues who trust each other, sometimes in risky situations in soup kitchens. If a young man wears the garb, imitates the mannerisms, and invests in artifacts associated with a controversial rock star, he is manifesting an "assemblage of culture-traits and complexes regularly found together." If he should appear in a tuxedo and play classical recitals, he would give signs that he has moved into the endangered classical musician culture.

If a young woman dresses in a Harley-Davidson jacket along with ragged jeans and displays her pierced tongue and tattooed arms, we are meant to deduce the culture to which she belongs. When she tidies up for a senior high job fair or interviews with a company where she is seeking employment, she has stepped into the sphere of corporate culture. If a person consistently behaves in a jarring and cynical manner, we can assume that we will not see him at an evangelical campus group

---

5. Bagby, *Culture and History*, pp. 104-5.

meeting. If it looks as though I am stereotyping some "ideas, knowledge, beliefs, norms, and values," note that the participants in the cultures just described *want* to be stereotyped, since they have been signaling what kind of culture they have chosen. Of course, no iron hand grips them and places them in one culture and not another. No authorities need to encourage relationships based on trust in one or make chaos of them in another. Individuals often remain free to shatter stereotypes, to change their ways and their communities. But normally it is the business of members of a culture to meet the terms of a group, even though they remain free to transcend "irregularly."

We may speak of a culture of trust when there is evidence that through internal or external means the religious, political, economic, artistic, scientific, technological, educational, and linguistic expressions of a group lead participants to count on each other and keep commitments. Since a variety of components of a culture of trust can be strengthened and new ones can be developed, it will be our business to observe these processes in a number of areas. Three will stand out, including the two already mentioned — namely, science and religion. We will add a third, the arena of *public life,* where citizens perceive potential or actual breakdowns of trust. The members of each of these cultures, along with their own subcultures, have it in their power to make some progress in resisting the chaos and corruption that go with broken trust and in helping build cultures of trust. But doing so puts them at risk.

CHAPTER 2

Seven Levels Where Risk and Trust Meet

N o one can speak intelligently about trust without dealing with its inevitable accompanying theme: risk. We take different kinds of risks depending on the encounters we expect. Athletes who have trusted their coaches and schedulers still risk injury or humiliation whenever they step out on the field or floor for games. Patients who trust their physicians who have offered good counsel along with medication still take the risk that something could go wrong, given the complexity of their bodies and the diseases that afflict them. There is no sure thing in such situations. Certainly, the honest investment counselor wisely advises that in all investments, since they deal with unknown futures, there is also no sure thing. Whoever enters a debate takes the risk of losing the argument or losing perspective if she wins it. For that matter, in the context of "building cultures," as this book describes the acts, people take risks upon entering the "universe of discourse" or the "world" of their conversation partner. They play the game of seeing where a conversation will go, and it can go to places that will reveal their vast pools of ignorance on many subjects. This will occur most of all when they have to speak about something that goes beyond their experience or thrives beyond their own competences and specialties. Risk goes with the trust territory.

Just as trust is an issue on many levels of life, and risk accompanies it, whoever wants to make sense of the place of trust will be prepared to encounter it on many levels or in different ranges, beginning with close to home.

First: Within the Self, the Basis in "Soul"

In the mind and heart and gut of anyone who bids for trust, then, calculating risk is a key element, whether in extending or receiving trust. If the future were known, there would be no need for trust — or risk. Taking a risk on another person or an institution means assessing both one's own interior life and external experiences with respect to those of the other. The members of cultures and subcultures that are to be built have to be taken as individuals, with whom talk of trust begins. It is almost banal to observe that one trusts a person who possesses integrity, gains a reputation for that possession or manifestation, and amasses a record of action consistent with that reputation. In our context, the human soul is the first element in the building block set in place by individuals. However, the concept of *soul* is so often taken for granted and treated casually that one cannot creatively use it without explaining what one intends with the word. I choose it here in an effort to show that issues of trust are more than passing, more than "bone deep."

Secular uses often associate or even equate the "soul" with "the spiritual," and thus they are in danger of seeing it broadened to the point that it becomes pointlessly vague. Religious usages rely on languages of faith, which in many cases evoke Platonic concepts such as "the immortality of the soul." These uses are not what I mean by "soul" here. In Platonism the body was the prison house for the soul, and such a soul demanded its own kind of attention, little of which has a bearing on our question of trust.

In Western culture the evocation of "soul" has admittedly drawn more on these Platonic references than on Hebrew Scripture or the New Testament, where there is little talk of an immortal soul. "[God] alone . . . has immortality . . ." (1 Tim. 6:16). Yet, with amazing frequency, expressions of Christian piety encourage belief that the soul is an invisible factor or agency in the physical make-up of a person. In such a view, soul exists in combination with or in contrast to the body. Materialists, of course, find it easy to dismiss these in both the Platonic and Jewish or Christian understandings. In the biology of the brain or any part of the body, where, they ask, is "soul" located? When that question was posed, many philosophers and theologians who were devoted to the concept of soul scrambled to find some locations of this invisible feature or organ. They usually made a laughingstock of themselves because they could find no organic or electric residue that could be called "soul." If the concept endured, its survival usually was metaphorical or poetic.

Now, on the issue of trust and trustworthiness: deciding on which side of the debates one settles while discussing "soul" has little bearing on the question of what human feature most contributes to the understanding of character, integrity, and trustworthiness, or which of these appear to be integrally linked. Instead, what has to be discussed is any "agency" of human life that relates to matters of trust, on one hand, or that sabotages any attempt to build character and help someone become trustworthy, on the other. Given that need, how shall we speak of soul?

An exploration that has been helpful comes from my former colleague Leon Kass, of the University of Chicago. In an essay on the development of soul, Kass depends in part on Aristotle — just as I depend on both Aristotle and Kass.

> By soul I mean nothing mystical or religious, not a disembodied spirit or person, not one of Homer's shades or anything else that departs the body intact, not a ghost in a machine or a pilot in a ship, not, indeed, a "thing" at all.... I understand by soul the integrated vital powers of a naturally organic body, always possessed by such a body while it is alive ("animated," "ensouled"), even when such powers are not actively at work (e.g., in sleep or before maturation).... All living things have soul.... The ascent of soul has meant the possibility both of an ever-greater awareness of and openness *to* the world, and an ever-greater freedom *in* the world. The hierarchy of soul is a hierarchy of openness and purposiveness.[1]

I lift out ten elements from that paragraph. First, one trusts the person who comes across as being *integrated,* which means that the various expressions of her humanness interrelate creatively. It is difficult to trust someone who is not integrated or who might be dis-integrating, which would mean that her mental properties and actions are chaotic. This does not mean that we must forget all bases for trust when someone's "vital powers" are not integrated. Nietzsche observed, in his oft-quoted "mantra" in the prologue to *Thus Spake Zarathustra,* that "one must still

---

1. Leon Kass, *Toward a More Natural Science: Biology and Human Affairs* (New York: Free Press, 1985), pp. 272-75.

have chaos in oneself in order to give birth to a dancing star." That dictum may work well with artists; yet, in the normal course of human affairs, a person tends to look for integrated character. One who finds it in another or others while reaching for trust can find consistency, some measure of constancy, and regularity, or predictability.

Kass's second descriptive term further advances the concept of trustworthiness in the elements of soul. It would not occur to a person to describe someone as soulful or embodying soul were he not *vital.* In fact, a new corpse may bear most features of a living being: the shape, the volume, the sinews and corpuscles are there for a short time after death. But they do not add up to anything one would call soul. Analogically, of course, we may speak of a poem or a painting or a sculpture as being vital. This, in our context, has a bearing on whether it is thought to have the integrating character, or to evoke the sense of trust, that "animated" art does. In most human transactions, however, one assumes and recognizes that the "other" is alive and capable of being wounded or able to give assurances and comfort. When this *anima* is weak or absent, as in the case of a person who is apathetic or who suffers from *acedia* (described by medieval theologians as expressing sadness in the face of spiritual good), there is no occasion for trusting. How could such a person find the motive or energy to deliver on his part of any bargain in the give-and-take of a trust relationship?

The concept of "soul" is again relevant with respect to the noun where the "integrated" and the "vital" meet in *powers.* In this case, as in other cases, how the feature is exercised is in no small way an element in what inspires a response of trust. If I invest "trust" in another person, I expect him to deliver some kind of response. One serves a comatose relative with acts of love, hand-holding, and the delivery of palliatives. It is even possible to speak of trust in the patient's ability to survive and recover; but such survival and recovery are of interest in the assessment of trust only when sufficient powers are present for there to be responses. Some of these can be as weak as the squeeze of a comforter's hand or a whisper in a dying person's ear. All moves that are designed to enhance trust rely on the powers and the empowerment of all who are involved in transactions. Even expressions of apparent weakness can be powers that evoke trust, as these are exemplified in the innocent person who is condemned to death. They may also be manifest in the strong person whose strength is limited by the bars of a prison. Martin Luther King, Jr., was never more vital, alive, and powerful than when he was confined to a prison. So it is appropriate to speak of trusting the one who exercises power in weakness or within limits, but it would be a strange expression if one connected trust with the utter absence of power, which takes definitive form in death.

Kass speaks, fourth, of soul as being a feature of "a *naturally* organic body." One must pause for a moment in the face of the adverb "naturally." In matters involving the giving and receiving of trust, it may often be the case that one has to do some prompting and pushing. It is not "natural" for a relaxed body to step up to activity. However, the one who trusts or is to be trusted is normally observed and spoken of as a person who has engaged in trust-bearing activities so consistently that he becomes "natural."

The adverb "naturally" connects with what is a fifth mark, the adjective *organic,* as in "an organic body." Both descriptions are associated with the first term, "integrated." Writers as ancient as the Stoics and the apostle Paul observe the loss of the integrated or organic character of a person when a part is severed from the main body. Paul's classic description of this in 1 Corinthians 12 is a passage worth citing for believer and nonbeliever alike in our present context because of how well it points to the "organic" feature of soul. The reader does well to ask whether one can extend trust to a detached "member" of the body, which, being cut off — and because it is cut off — plays no part in "soul."

One way to do this is to ask, during the Pauline register of body parts in 1 Corinthians 12, whether one can trust the detached hand or ear or eye or nose, the head or feet? Actually — and again metaphorically — in society as well as in the individual body, one has to count on the organic character of something or someone to develop: one trusts if the other fulfills the function for which it is intended. I trust my banker if she delivers on the terms of our financial covenant; I do not have to trust whether she will sing in tune at a concert. I trust my governor if he faithfully follows the terms of his civil oath and performs duties connected with it, without having to trust him to serve aces in tennis. If a public servant were to claim that the ability to sing on key or to deliver a fierce tennis serve would qualify her or him for public office, I would appraise the song or the serve independently, because it is not connected organically with the person who fulfills a different role in different occasions.

Sixth, Kass speaks of soul as being connected with an organic *body.* Body here represents "the other" as a being or an agent who confronts a person in tangible or palpable ways. One can trust a book that evokes integrity; but the book does so because an author has written it, and the reader makes an assessment about trust in the light of that bodily whole. If there is known fakery or breaking of trust by the author, the book suffers and is dismissed. In recent years there have been exposures of deceptive authors who have falsely written about invented experiences in order to make their books alluring, engrossing, and believable. After the exposure of an author, it is almost impossible to read on. If the author had written fiction, no one would be disappointed or enraged to find out that the events in the book did not happen — at least not as described. The novelist wins trust by the way she fulfills her art. The memoirist wins trust if the events he describes match the realities as they are available for examination by readers.

The four other aspects of "soul" that we are connecting with integrity and trustworthiness have a different character. First, they must represent and promise *possibility*. In Kass's case, this means "the possibility of an ever-greater awareness of and openness *to* the world and an ever-greater freedom *in* the world." This phrase demonstrates why the integrity of the soul matters so much when one speaks of trust. Cut off the possibility of openness to the world and freedom in the world, and you are left with no occasions to trust and no one to engage trustingly. Next, we put ourselves more readily into the hands of someone who shows "an ever-greater *freedom* in the world." This awareness suggests an imagination that can be counted on to deal with problems and offer promises, and the openness is something we count on when seeking solutions to matters that elicit trust.

Finally, "the hierarchy of soul is a hierarchy of *openness* and *purposiveness*." Openness is necessary because trust always involves risk, and the one who trusts or is to be trusted has to be open to risk. Meanwhile, the element of purposiveness seals the matter of trustworthiness. One is inclined to trust an individual, community, or institution if it indicates some direction and investment in the future. Trust is always involved with the future.

Second: The Self and the Immediate Other

Ticking off a list of features described by a contemporary physician-philosopher, Leon Kass, as I have just done, can help clarify some aspects of trust and the giving of trust, which is an important step in un-covering or recovering it in contemporary circumstances. When seek-ing to build trust in trust itself, virtually every philosopher who deals with the subject or everyone who promotes it begins by saying that the first nurturing ground and test of trust is the individual. Yet the think-ers and advocates also converge on the communal factor. Trust is a key indicator of character, and the acquisition and nurture of character and of a community of character always implies and encourages attention to some form of community.

This attention is necessary since the cultivation of integrity, charac-ter, and a community of trust is neither automatic nor uncomplicated. For a variety of reasons, we do not take at face value the assurances of trust. The first of these derives from the fact that honest people may not know themselves, even when they engage in lifelong examinations of themselves to assess their own trustworthiness. Arthur Frank, in *The Renewal of Generosity,* brings up this subject implicitly when he uses as his epigraph and guiding theme a judgment in the form of a charge by Marcus Aurelius: "You've wandered all over and finally realized that you never found what you were after: how to live."[2] Self-reflection shows up in all kinds of revealing phrases. Faced with a potential dilemma, you may well say, as so many others have, "I'm not sure if I can trust myself enough to. . . ." Then follows an internal inventory, a message to one's self that takes the form of questioning: Is my record of being faithful strong enough that I can count on it? That others can? How does one measure trust subjectively?

For that reason, most counsel about fidelity and trust urges that the solitary thinker place herself in some context of friends, associates, al-lies, fellow believers, alumni groups, or others who can help an individ-ual measure the evidences of trust through a period of years. Along with the reinforcement, goading, and inspiration of one's community, there are representations of the self by "the other," of the kind seen in media coverage, evaluations produced for portfolios, or overheard lockerroom exchanges: "You can't trust that guy any further than you can throw his agent. Unless there is a notarized signature, forget about him." Or: "She's as good as her word. She does not even need to extend a hand for a shake, or even say a word. Her record is clear." In the age of the Internet,

---

2. Arthur Frank, *The Renewal of Generosity: Illness, Medicine, and How to Live* (Chi-cago: University of Chicago Press, 2004), p. 1.

links such as "MySpace" and "Facebook" allow ordinarily anonymous people to experiment with some measure of exposure, but still one that is of a kind that can remain anonymous and thus remain most subject to distortion and self-inflation. The presence of such sites or links, it must be said, also reveals new methods for deceiving. As a result, they have inspired an industry of those who act out their suspicions by saying: "Don't believe anything, certainly not everything, that someone on the web says about himself. Be doubly sure that you check him out!" And that veil of anonymity is another reason for advising that individuals be connected and involved with communities of various kinds, which serve to break down isolation and form circles of those who can contribute to and test the professions of trust and trustworthiness.

Third: Where Teaching Trust Can Occur

For the majority of adult citizens who are placed in situations where public trust is expected and demanded, the experience of higher education is a key to development. It helps to have been brought up in a family and other close-up forms of community that nurtured trust. The formation of character, the deepening of integrity, and the basis for trust do not begin for an individual at age eighteen or beyond. Every developmental stage plays its part, and those who sing the praises of someone who has proven to be trustworthy usually assess the background of the admired person, a background that portrays parent-child, adult-child, and child-child interaction as they relate to trust. Still, maturation during college and university education at their best provide an opportunity for critical reflection and development.

Teachers play major roles, and how they go about teaching matters. This will show up in the way a teacher opens up for questions: she has to trust that someone will have an answer, or the class session breaks down. One of the best reflections on the teaching process that can inform our exploration of the development of trust is that of a Canadian professor, Northrop Frye, a longtime observer of the classroom transaction.[3] Not for him are patterns that do not allow for person-to-person interaction. Among those patterns are "distance learning" and computer-based education: they may have a place in education, but

---

3. Northrop Frye, *The Great Code* (New York: Harcourt Brace Jovanovich, 1982), p. xv.

they are not of much import in education for integrity and trust. The computerized lecture and visual display, followed by testing conveyed by the Internet, do not allow for meaningful "I-Thou" personal interaction. Without this personal dimension, the development of character and the enrichment of trust-relations have to be accidental or must occur extracurricularly. Ideally, the development that I am speaking of here goes on in small seminars or classes, where the teacher and all the members are exposed to each other, can playfully incite others to action, and can then be moved by the others.

Picture the student who has through his early years gained some knowledge of moral issues relating to trust but has not put them together or related them to his personal philosophy. Now he is in a liberal arts class setting. In Frye's framing of the experience, notice first the teacher and her role: "The teacher is someone who attempts to re-create the subject in the student's mind." The teacher does not start from scratch, but builds on what she trusts has gone before. A student who habitually cheated in high school brings less lore and learning to higher education than will the one who had to make his way honestly, and in that honesty developed integrity almost to the point that it becomes habitual.

The good teacher quickly discerns that even poorly educated young adults who open themselves to higher education, usually with the pursuit of vocation in mind, have some "raw material in the brain," some half-formed but often unconnected bits of learning. Building on the teacher's perception and assessment is a strategy. Frye continues: "And his or her strategy in doing this is first of all to get the student to recognize what he already potentially knows. . . ." Such knowing involves both "knowing that," in the form of data, and "knowing how," which means knowing so that what has been learned is ready to be stored, processed, and put to work in new ways. To speak of the student's "potentially knowing," as Frye does, sounds a bit strange: if one potentially knows something, he already knows. But Frye is right: most "potential knowing" refers to glimmers and reminiscences, tentative proposals, risks, and achievements on which the transaction with the teacher builds.

Now, if the teacher has been portrayed as being trustworthy and is conscious of the need to develop trust, she can risk something that is integral to the learning process but not always welcome among those who feel they "have it made." They consider that they know enough "that's" and have tried enough of the "how's" to prosper. Therefore, the teacher has to be probing and aggressive without turning destructively invasive. Here is how Frye puts it: The next step for the teacher as she relates to the student "includes breaking up the powers of repression in his mind that keep him from knowing what he knows. . . ." Such repression can have occurred because the learner has invested in the trust of another person — a parent, friend, coach, or other teacher — and then had that trust betrayed. But at the crucial moment the victim was directed to someone who could point to new resources for developing trust, and could provide new experiences that would foster them. So the student has a carryover of repressions that have to be shattered, because they produce barriers that have to be broken down or broken up. When such breaking occurs, says Frye, the student has a chance to advance "knowing what he knows."

Then comes the cinching line that brings onstage the familiar key element in trusting: risk. "That is why it is the teacher, rather than the student, who asks most of the questions." Any teacher has asked often enough, "Any questions?" and been met with stunning silence. Such an experience calls for another strategy, the one Frye advocates, a strategy as old as Plato or Erasmus: the teacher asks the questions. Now there is freedom to explore the development and expression of trust in others, usually people whose writings or achievements are being studied. A leading question, taking off from Marcus Aurelius, would be: "Have you learned how to live?"

Fourth: In Community as Conventionally Conceived

Teachers who ask questions and help students find answers about how to live as trustworthy or in trust often ask their classes to carry their learning self-consciously and then with a focus on what community means in matters of trust. This is true because trust always means having confidence in the "other," and that learning to place confidence can only happen in the face of the other. The French novelist Stendhal reduced the issues of trust, integrity, and character to a single point in his aphorism: "One can acquire everything in solitude — except character." That claim may not be the whole of it; for example, you cannot catch contagious diseases in solitude. But being apprentices in the trust-giving and trust-receiving relationship involves being learners with oth-

26

ers who can work out differences about trust and work in steps about learning trust.

This observation, of course, implies that one is in contact with the right kind of friends and "others." It means calling for a higher level of interaction than is presupposed in the jocular colloquialism "he hangs out with a bunch of characters." People of character, just like "characters," do come in bunches. Admire someone for keeping a covenant, and she is likely to respond to questions about how and why she makes and keeps commitments, with likely references to family, childhood friends, mentoring adults, and fellow parishioners. But much credit will also go to the questioning teacher, the one who creates a climate for growth.

One story can serve to remind us of how devoid of potential such "hanging out" is, a tale dragged up from the barrels of motivational addresses I've heard through the years. It happened that a frontiersman in unsettling times in the wild west of long ago was arrested for being a horse thief. Naturally, despite all the evidence of purloined horses on hand, the person detained, when asked to plead innocent or guilty, immediately shouted the predictable "I am innocent."

Question two, then: Do you want to be tried by a judge or a "jury of your peers?"

Peers? What or who are they? When he heard the explanation — "Peers are people just like you!" — the self-proclaimed innocent reflected for a split second and then snorted, "What, me be tried by a bunch of horse thieves?"

Had he been a human services volunteer or an exemplary citizen, he would have welcomed peers in the seat of justice. As a matter of fact, he himself would not likely have been a suspect, for he would not be tempted to be a horse thief at all. Had he "hung out" through the years with fellows who knew right from wrong and everyone knew that they knew it, he would have taken his risks for judgment on a randomly selected jury. To say that one can acquire everything in solitude except character gets sharpened: one *can* develop trustworthiness in company, and in community one will need it in some form or other.

The experience of community, properly cultivated, is a great aid in building cultures of trust. However, community is difficult to achieve. Many analysts of culture define community as a setting in which people can share some secrets, can confide, can rely on each other. For many, the immediate and then the extended families might serve as the most intimate communities. They cannot prosper if there is not a high level of trust among the members. However, the infamous "in-law" jokes, which sometimes exaggerate and often disguise harsh realities, demonstrate that at no level of common life is trust easy to attain. For others, whether the family has broken trust or whether such an up-close community enhances it, the circle of friends can provide community. Here again, "friend" is almost by definition "someone who trusts me and whom I trust." Yet the betrayal of trust in friendships is so frequent a phenomenon that novelists can count on the story of such breaches for an easily recognizable plot line. Friendships often become ex-friendships. Local religious congregations, especially if they are relatively small, can provide person-to-person community; those who choose to be lifelong members of such congregations testify to their richness, and they are reinforced by a sense of divine sanction. However, "church fights," beginning on the local level, are legendary and were evident as early as in the letters of the apostle Paul. Folklore about synagogue tensions animates many Jewish stories. Community? You can't live without it, when seeking to trust; but you can't easily live with it either.

Glenn Tinder's writings on this subject have informed me since he published *Community: Reflections on a Tragic Ideal* in 1980. As I reread it with the topic of trust in mind, I found it as fresh and shocking as before. It has forced me to use the word "community" cautiously and tentatively, as though placing it in quotation marks.

> Community is not only alluring, . . . however, it is also unattainable. Man is not capable of community — not, at least, in any full and stable form. No doubt relationships of communal quality can be realized occasionally and in limits by a family, a town, a university, or even a nation. But no historical institution can be purely and simply a community.
>
> Full community is unattainable partly because man is a natural being; he lives in space and time, and he dies. To a surprising extent man's spatial, temporal, and moral nature is ignored in writings on community.
>
> Even so, our natural capacity for community is often far in excess of our moral capacity. The tendency of every person to subordinate everything to his own pleasure and preeminence — a tendency that is subtle and enduring, although often disguised — frequently forecloses whatever communal possibilities nature offers.

28

The natural question comes to mind: If all this is true, how could anyone invest in community?

> To say that man is spatial, temporal, and mortal, after all, is to say that he is finite, and this implies that the natural values he embodies are limited both in degree and duration. . . . If there are any who achieve moral perfection they are so rarely encountered in daily life as to be irrelevant to the problem of community. In sum, no one commands more than qualified respect. The communal impulse capable of fulfillment only with those one respects and only in proportion to one's respect for them, is correspondingly inhibited.[4]

An answer to the question I posed just before that last Tinder paragraph might be: people invest in community because they must. In the course of a life, they will be — and, unless deluded, they will know that they will be — frustrated in many endeavors and perhaps blinded by some half-successes that they will label "community." But the dream of community needs to be surrounded by other aspirations toward other social forms. They can also be what I am portraying as building blocks in the effort to develop cultures of trust. Those who would develop them need some halfway stops or bridging points between themselves in isolation and the larger society.

Fifth: The Places of Intermediation

Even many scholars who analyze the subject and come up with dour observations and expectations about community do not despair. They move on and reframe the issue. In sociologist Robert Nisbet's terms, they come up with something he calls "intermediation." They provide the next forms that go into the building of cultures of trust. "Major groups which fall in between the individual and the sovereign state are at once buffers against too arbitrary a political power and reinforcements to the individual's conception of himself and his own powers."[5]

---

4. Glenn Tinder, *Community: Reflections on a Tragic Ideal* (Baton Rouge: Louisiana State University Press, 1980), pp. 136-37.

5. Robert Nisbet, *The Making of Modern Society* (New York: New York University Press, 1986), pp. 24-25.

Immanuel Kant's line about human crookedness and yet the implied need for construction also reinforces the idea of human frailty: "Out of timber so crooked as that from which man is made nothing entirely straight can be built."[6] So the house of trust will sag and slope and shake in the storm, but the kind of shelter it offers is still better than none. So those who agree with Tinder's and Kant's observations tend to move on with Nisbet to find linked timbers that can be used to continue building.

Those who are called to engage in criticism or to bring experts and specialists and, for that matter, the nonprofessional public together, know how difficult the tasks of "intermediation" are. If one is building cultures of trust out of subcultures of trust, or relating these cultures to each other, one has to know that the mediator is always vulnerable to attacks from all parties. Thus a scientist who is called to engage in dialogue with a scholar of religion or anyone who has informed interests in religion needs the trust of other scientists if she is to be credible. This does *not* mean that scientists have to agree with her — only that they implicitly grant her permission to take on the risks of misunderstanding. Similarly, when there are religiously involved attempts by anyone to engage in conversation with scientists, the religiously oriented participant knows he will be met with suspicion by many believers and practitioners in religious fields. And the intermediator knows that people on all sides of the science/religion divides can be suspicious when the inquiry or conversation moves out of the laboratory or sacristy into the public zone. There one often meets wariness or hears carping because such a level of bridging in popular terms can lead to hurtful compromise. Or, to those who will not take risks, it can imply the bartering away of quality that can be more likely achieved, they think, in isolation or with the company of "like with like."

Sixth: The Patterns of Association and the Heightening of Risk

If we were cautious when speaking of "community," there is reason now to be more bold when proposing the word "association." It is the preferred generic term used today to indicate a distinctive but highly di-

6. Immanuel Kant, "Idee zu einer allgemeinen Geschichte in weltbürgerlicher Absicht," in *Kant's Gesammelte Schriften* (Berlin, 1912), vol. 8, p. 23.

verse form of human association. It is, emphatically, key wherever people would build cultures of trust. When they set out to do so, they allow
for intermediation of subgroups and help enrich the relationship of all
to authorities, which do not by nature breed community. Such builders
allow for self-preservative action, which is based in part on pragmatic
experiment, and which is adjustable. All of this has to be present in order for trust and cultures of trust to grow.

I know of no better illustration of this move or form than the parable of porcupines, creatures who make metaphorical appearances in
my argument from time to time. Pessimistic philosopher Arthur
Schopenhauer told it, and as retold here by Michael Oakeshott, it deserves full quotation.

> There was once, so Schopenhauer tells us, a colony of porcupines.
> They were wont to huddle together on a cold winter's day and, thus
> wrapped in communal warmth, escape being frozen. But, plagued
> with the pricks of each other's quills, they drew apart. And every time
> the desire for warmth brought them together again, the same calam-
> ity overtook them. Thus they remained, distracted between two mis-
> fortunes, able neither to tolerate nor to do without one another, until
> they discovered that when they stood at a certain distance from one
> another they could both delight in one another's individuality and
> enjoy one another's company. They did not attribute any metaphysi-
> cal significance to this distance, nor did they imagine it to be an inde-
> pendent source of happiness, like finding a friend. They recognized
> it to be a relationship in terms not of substantive enjoyments but of
> contingent considerabilities that they must determine for them-
> selves. Unknown to themselves, they had invented civil association.[7]

Every line of this parable suggests some elements in the building of
cultures of trust. Individuals suffer on their figuratively cold winter
days, and they need the help of others. If they overinvest in trust, they
experience frustration and even pain, and they draw back into the isolation born of mistrust: no one wants to get hurt. The natural reaction,
then, is to "remain distracted" and to suffer for that. As the experiences
of trust become more frequent, they grow sufficiently confident to draw

---

7. Arthur Schopenhauer, *Parerga and Paralipomena: Short Philosophical Essays*, vol. 2,
trans. E. F. J. Payne (Oxford: Clarendon, 1974), pp. 651-52.

closer together and offer and receive trust. So, without profound metaphysical bases for community, Oakeshott proposes, the porcupines find a range for developing confidence in each other and the group.

In the eighteenth-century sense of the term, they had an "affection" for each other. This was not the kind of affection that gets displayed on valentines or Hallmark cards. Instead, it means that they shared an "affective" experience of life. Thomas Jefferson, in the first draft of the Declaration of Independence, used the term in that sense when he spoke of nurturing a republic marked by affection.[8] This meant that citizens, he hoped, were going to remain bonded through their recall of the experience of the War of Independence, during which colonials had to trust each other in spite of their differences; and now, having survived it, they would give expression to affection while forming the new nation. It may sound strange to compare the porcupines' discovery to this affective range, but by making the comparison, I intend to help provoke an awareness of the momentary and fragile instruments that can be used for the building of trust.

The philosophical image that comes to mind for patterns in which different expressions of trust or, conversely, lapses into mistrust occur — we might think of it as a loose pattern of institutionalizing culture — is from a Dutch Calvinist political scientist named Johannes Althusius (1557-1638). He spoke of a model called *communitas communitatum,* and of its constituents as *symbiotes,* who, in living off each other, feed each other. "The public association exists when many private associations are linked together for the purpose of establishing an inclusive political order. It can be called a community, an associated body, or the pre-eminent political association." I like to speak of the civil order itself or as a whole as being an "association of associations." As the base or level moves beyond "self" and "other" and "community" to "association," cultures of trust become ever harder to build, but any achievement on this level offers greater public benefit. Althusius at this point is reflecting Aristotle, who spoke of the *polis* as an "aggregate of many members." He goes on to criticize Socrates, who propounded "a false notion of unity from which he starts." Aristotle thought there should be unity "both of the family and of the state, but in some respects only." Trust within the former has a "community" base, but on the level of the

---

8. Garry Wills, *Inventing America: Jefferson's Declaration of Independence* (Garden City, NY: Doubleday, 1978), pp. 312-14; see also pp. 273-83.

whole *polis,* the effort to effect it would be destructive. We would call the effort utopian, while realizing that it could easily become dystopian. Utopias are built on assumptions about human planning that assume that risks among citizens would be low and trust hardly necessary. However, Aristotle contends, "We ought not to attain this greatest unity even if we could, for it would be the destruction of the state." We may often speak of "the national community" or "the American community," but this language has to be figurative. If trust is to be based on a "harmony [turned] into mere unison" then "it would be the destruction of the state," and the built culture would come crashing down.[9]

Another metaphor for the "association of associations," forms of social life that had begun in intimate community but did not remain there, comes from Edmund Burke, who speaks of "platoons" or, with less military connotation, "inns."

> We begin our public affections in our families. No cold relation is a zealous citizen. We pass on to our neighborhoods, and our habitual provincial connections. These are inns and resting-places. Such divisions of our country have been formed by habit, and not by a sudden jerk of authority; where so many little images of the great country in which the heart found something which it could fill. The love to the whole is not extinguished by this subordinate partiality.[10]

Seventh: Where Stories Get Told and Heard

Two more elements have to be introduced in the arenas or zones of action: story and custom. Key features of trust in the intermediatory zone is the story and the act of storytelling. Stories of betrayal or victimization undercut efforts to build elements of cultures of trust. Stories of heroism and faithfulness among humans who keep to the customs and covenants of trust inspire ever more trust. They point to the exemplary, to the embodied heroic virtues in ordinary people, and they can inspire

9. See Frank S. Carney, ed. and trans., *The Politica of Johannes Althusius* (Indianapolis: Liberty Fund, 1998), pp. 17, 28, 39, and 207-8, for elaborations on this concept, including the concept of *symbiotes.*

10. Edmund Burke, *Reflections on the Revolution in France* (1790; New York: Penguin Books, 1986), pp. 243-44.

emulation among many in the subcultures they are meant to redeem or enhance.

Whether the stories are passed on among the generations, in classrooms, or in public media, their transmission has been, is, and can continue to be a major way for building cultures of trust. The public reads stories of broken trust, as in the business world or professional sports. Uninterpreted, these accounts can lower the possibilities for trust-relations as the public grows first suspicious and then cynical. But it is also demonstrable that telling the stories of those who keep trust can inspire others to consider trust. They can also demonstrate expressions of trust and reasons for it grounded in custom and habit. And telling the stories helps people who exist in cultures distant from each other and hostile to them to learn empathy. Trust grows.

I have witnessed an American Jew, defending the policies of present-day Israel in the face of critics, say in frustration or resignation: "You'll not understand what it is like to be a Jew or an Israeli, in the face of assaults and terrorism, which have forced us to build settlements and walls and road-blocks! The problem is, *you've never heard our story!*" Then, a moment later, someone else at that conference table, someone whose ancestry had not been an issue or even a point of illustration, spoke up and complained: "And *you* have never heard our story. My grandfather was a Palestinian farmer who was forced to sell and vacate his farm in 1948 at the birth of Israel." On one of those scenes, the two, newly aware of what stories unheard can do to perpetuate mistrust, and now seeing some hope for shared stories, agreed to meet to converse, not to argue. In that process they were setting two figurative stones in the building of trust. Of course, they have not "settled" things in zones where killing and the building of walls has gone on; but they have removed one barrier against the efforts to move toward better situations.

On another occasion, when a foundation gathered representatives of groups or causes known to be hostile to each other for a seminar, a high official in a conservative, family-oriented group was criticizing gay and lesbian couples for what "gay marriage" would do to other forms of marriage. Someone asked him, "What does someone else's marriage — same-sex in this case — do to undercut traditional heterosexual couples in their marriages?" He answered with a litany of woes that he contended accompanied homosexual practices: cruising, pornography, rape, child abuse, and the like. Across the table from him was a representative of one of the causes or agencies, a woman who "happened to be," as the saying goes, in a lesbian relationship for years. On the verge of tears, she burst out that she and her partner were faithful to each other, were good parents to two children, were law-abiding citizens, were engaged in voluntary activities, and were church members to boot. The man across from her had offended her deeply, and she held back her tears only because she was busy suppressing her anger. "You've never heard our story," she said to him when he said, "I've never met one of your kind before."

A moment later a self-described "pro-life evangelical feminist" intervened, assuming that the previous female testifier was likely to receive much support in this gathering. "Now you liberals have had your story told. Here's mine: I think most of you would admire my life, my calling, my commitments, my philosophy in many respects — but not my opposition to abortion. Because of my theology, outlook, and commitment, I cry every night thinking of the several thousand innocents who lost their life before birth today. I won't call abortion 'murder,' but it is killing, and I think it's wrong." The representative of a "pro-choice" organization seated across from her was taken aback. She had begun to admire this new acquaintance before she heard her testimony, and now she came close to saying, "I've never met one of your kind up close." She had never heard that story before.

I was later told that these four conferees might have agreed to meet to converse someday soon thereafter. Again, one does not anticipate the conversion of any of the four to the camp of his or her counterpart. This is not the point at such gatherings. The point is that "the other as stranger" now becomes "the other as conversation partner and friend," each one undoubtedly no less committed to his or her cause than before, but at least now empathic and ready to listen and then to speak again. The four represented here were bringing their stories to a scene in which they have bought more time and created a climate wherein another part of a culture of trust can be supported.

Since historians are professional tellers of stories, the witness of a notable one is informative. Gerda Lerner reminds historians, and all of us, of this:

> By tracing one's personal roots and grounding one's identity in some collectivity with a shared past — be that collectivity defined by race, sex, class, ethnicity, religion, or nationality — one acquires stability

and the basis for community. . . . Without history, no nation can enjoy legitimacy or patriotic allegiance.

Referring to the work of historian-storytellers as teachers, Lerner continues:

> Above all, we seek to tell a story and tell it well — to hold the audience's attention and to seduce it — by one means or another, into suspending disbelief and inattention. We seek to focus concentrated attention upon ourselves and to hold it long enough to allow the students' minds to be directed into unexpected pathways and to perceive new patterns.[11]

Lerner, at that time the president of the Organization of American Historians, could have been written off by critics as a mere organization woman who was out to parade the relevancies of her profession and was not speaking about trust in particular. Yet in those few sentences she was pointing to one of the agencies for building trust that goes far beyond the classroom, the library, or the rarefied interfaith seminar.

The word "rarefied" jolted me a bit as I typed it, and it may serve to remind readers of at least four things they might be likely to bring up if our imagined conversation turned real. First, these illustrations are drawn from structured circumstances, often settings in which participants have had to lay down their arms, because the law or the spirit of a gathering forced them to. Second, in the teaching scene, the classmate ethos is intolerant of the intolerant. In the conference setting, activist participants are taking the day off from their usual refusal to acknowledge values held by others — or to acknowledge others at all. What good does it do, we may ask, on such a site to make the development of trust easy, especially if participants in these observed settings subsequently have to go back to neighborhoods where trust is rare? They will switch on the cable television provocateurs, who make their living creating suspicion and generating mistrust of all who are not of their party or ideology.

11. Gerda Lerner, "The Necessity of History and the Professional Historian," in *The Vital Past: Writings on the Uses of History,* ed. Stephen Vaughn (Athens, GA: University of Georgia Press, 1985); see esp. pp. 106, 108, 114-15.

We can acknowledge the value of all such questions and quibbles. This is not a how-to manual that offers detailed descriptions of the paths to cultures of trust (though I may sneak in a few how-to paragraphs at the book's end); rather, it is an attempt to bring some philosophical, theological, and certainly historical warrant for the value of such cultures, and to suggest that, against all odds, we humans who are normally mistrustful — witness our locks on vaults and our signed contracts — can, as individuals and in collectivities, begin to develop cultures of trust where there have never been any, or restore them where they have been devastated. Again, one must be modest about expectations. My theme throughout this book portrays incremental change. Citizens may be dazzled by utopian visions of trusting human collectivities or stunned by their counterparts, where trust is so rare as to seem absent. Or they can create examples, islands, templates, or beacons among people where trust becomes manifestly present, pragmatically effected, and representative of some of the ideals that are manifest in the stories we tell to our own groups and then to others.

A Major Concern for Mistrust Among Scientists and Religionists

It is in this sense that we can anticipate our major case study, which will focus on the cultures of suspicion that have come to develop among and between scientists and religionists. One can read or hear the story of scientists whose stories dwell on the persecutions of Galileo and Copernicus and uninformed critiques of Darwin to press the point that anyone possessing religious sensibilities should not be trusted, should be written off as ignorant, and should be opposed as an enemy of progress. Or, on the other side, one can hear or read the story of religious figures who point to the soulless declarations of many scientists. Even worse, one can hear the premature and violent rejections of anything termed religious. In militant corners of the scientific world, some best-selling authors, often called the "new atheists," dismiss all religions as purveyors of ignorance and irrelevant if not malicious censors of scientists.

On the other hand, one can hear and read scientists who are no less critical but who are differently informed, who write of their own struggles with faith, their own acknowledgment of the value of faith itself. Some of them raise scientific issues that need criticism, experiments that need to be aborted, or positive reports on their dialogues and seminars. Some of these emphasize the spiritual and churchly modes of experience and contribute to religious thinking and action for the common good.

The "new atheists" and the "fundamentalist creationists," representing opposite poles in the current polemics, share more than they might admit: they are making category mistakes in their effort to demolish "the other," and they are making noises that drown out the "conversation of humankind," which Michael Oakeshott, as I shall later detail, advances as the heart of liberal education.

Cultures of trust are built up over periods of many years by experimenters, meliorists, and those given to incremental gains. They can be harmed or destroyed very quickly and brutally. Their destruction has implications far beyond the local scenes or the specialized disciplines that at first glance are seen as isolated instances. If such cultures are born, developed, made use of, and protected, they connect symbiotically with other cultures. What we have addressed will not generate simple and open trust between the United States and Iran; it will not eliminate the need for police and locks or laws and contracts, nor will it provide models for top-to-bottom reform of mass media of communications or the worlds of commerce. Yet, even there, each step or example in building cultures of trust can produce positive consequences, as such efforts demonstrably have done in the past.

CHAPTER 3

Scripted Resources

O n the old observation that "you can't fight something with noth-ing," those who would fight for cultures of trust need "some-things" of their own, resources, ammunition, or, to fit better with our building metaphor, foundations and footings. They need to have some understanding of what trust itself means or can mean in particular con-texts. Another old observation or principle is: if you do not know furs, know your furrier, or if you do not know jewels, know your jeweler. The fact that both such professions, when they are fulfilled, are themselves based on trust-relations, is not the present point. That point reminds us that positive and profound views of what trust should look like are not constant in our cultures. Alert citizens can pick up some clues about trust as they discern the philosophies on which parents, teachers, min-isters, attorneys, and others — at their best — are drawing.

The first treasures to which our metaphorical furriers or jewelers will point, if they are experienced and have some sense of history and cultural nuance, will be religious. The religious elements may be dis-guised, half-forgotten, compromised, or even subjects of suspicion themselves. Yet they have provided much of the vocabulary of trust, taught basic lessons about discerning mistrust, and — again, at their best — informed and inspired people who seek to build cultures of trust.

This reference to religious resources does not imply that everyone who would contribute to cultures of trust has to profess a religion or be religious, by any of the prevalent definitions of religion or professions. In fact, many citizens today have felt betrayed specifically by religious institutions, some of whose professionals have broken trust. Some occasions for this breach are the widely publicized clerical abuse cases, the stories of financial scandals among evangelists, and the like. Members of the public may be merely disappointed that such institutions have not delivered on their promises. Even God can become an issue. When religion has meant belief in a provident God who beckons people to trust, but then seems to deny the confidence their prayers have shown, they ask where they can turn. Grant all the problems with religious trust, and you still are dealing with a culture in which millennia-old meanings are alive. After a natural disaster such as a hurricane or in the face of a personal or social crisis that is the result of human evil, such as 9/11 and other terrorist activity, interviewed survivors are quite open in their discussion of the ways God or humans broke trust. At the same time — and apparently paradoxically — others will speak of how and why they intensify their expressions of trust especially in the face of crises.

Among that vast majority of humans who do identify themselves as religious, or who "practice religion," there are some who announce that they are on spiritual searches or journeys. Others engage in formal studies and consistent ponderings of religious meanings, where religious understandings of trust underlie all others. People take oaths invoking the name of God, make pledges or promises of trust to each other in front of altars and with holy books open, or focus on trust in the solemn quiet of their private quarters. Long before the word "trust" traveled to agencies bannered as "savings and trust" banks or politicians advertised themselves as worthy of trust, people of all faiths were transacting on divine-human or human-to-human terms that are explicitly religious. Overlooking their traditions, habits, customs, and hopes would be a policy or practice that would doom much of any effort to build and sustain cultures of trust.

So extensive and profound are the positive ties connecting religion with trust that many scholars see the concept of trust itself to be at the heart of many religions. In the Christian tradition, witness to God as Love is predominant; but in Christian and Jewish *practice,* trust is prominent. It is integral to discourse on how God and humans relate and how humans are to express their love among their fellows. Trust is at the base of prayer, devotion, and worship. It becomes a prime subject for reflection by scholars and moralists in these traditions, though some may use cognate terms for it, such as "confidence" or, more regularly, "faith."

Faith as Trust, Trust as Faith

When historian of theology Jaroslav Pelikan was asked to write on "faith" for *The Encyclopedia of Religion,* he treated numerous subtopics in the "faith-as. . ." category, among them:

Faith-as-Faithfulness
Faith-as-Obedience
Faith-as-Dependence
Faith-as-Experience
Faith-as-Credo

"Faith-as-Trust" deals most directly with our theme. Drawing on the tradition for examples, Pelikan cites Martin Luther: "To 'have a god' is nothing else than to trust and believe in him with our whole heart," since "it is the trust and faith of the heart alone that makes both God and an idol." Pelikan elaborates:

> [T]he definition of faith-as-trust has been a way of focusing . . . expectation on the reliability of divine providence in both prosperity and failure: for good or ill, the ways of the divine will could be counted on, even though the details of their specific intent might not be discernible at any given moment. Such faith-as-trust even in the inscrutable goodness of the divine order presupposed a pattern of divine guidance in the past, which made it safe to conclude that there would be a continuity of such guidance into the future. Historically as well as psychologically, therefore, it is difficult to conceive of faith-as-trust in the absence of such a pattern, be it the outcome of the individual's own cumulative autobiography or of the history of the community to which the invitation has come to belong (or of both). Once established on the basis of this pattern of divine guidance, faith-as-trust has implied that the vicissitudes of the moment could not, or at any rate should not, undermine the confidence that ultimately the object of that trust would be vindicated.

Pelikan claims no Jewish or Christian monopoly for such a witness. He finds it also in the Greek tragedians, Muslim mystics, and writers such as Johann Wolfgang von Goethe, whose autobiography, *Dichtung und Wahrheit,* he cites. There faith-as-trust is simply faith: "Faith is a profound sense of security in regard to both the present and the future; and this assurance springs from confidence."[1]

Some philosophers of religion go so far as to note, as does Joseph J. Godfrey, S.J., that "trust is the heart of religion," a phrase he repeats in a survey of how "Vedantist, Buddhist, Hebrew, and Christian sacred writings point separately to a central role for trust." Godfrey goes on to quote Raymond Panikkar, who, after surveying "the religions of the world," proposes that trust — sometimes called "faith" — "is a dimension which is common to and indeed constitutive of all human beings." This he describes as "existential openness towards transcendence," or, at minimum, "existential openness" itself. This openness leads to the recognition that "nothing is capable of filling it, no 'human' value whatsoever can fill it up."

Godfrey tests his reasons for calling this "openness" and the responses to it "trust" by examining four dimensions of trusting that he calls *reliance, I-Thou trusting, security-trusting,* and *openness-trusting.* He finds them sufficiently present to give him confidence that his proposition that "trust is the heart of religion" stands up. Such typical conclusions from historians of religion provide confidence that religious meanings are central resources for anyone who would contribute to building cultures of trust.[2]

Why build? The task of constructing appears in a time when many speak of a crisis of trust in contemporary societies. Those who address these will find available a wide variety of definitions, assessments, resources, and strategies for approaching them. These range from unwarranted expressions of optimism to unhelpful expressions of pessimism, and from sweeping if abstract philosophical perspectives to close-up and minute practical counsels.

My approach deals with the hard-to-sustain middle range. From one side a person can hear claims that one-on-one, face-to-face encounters among individuals — as in "I don't trust you!" or "I trust you!" — will provide the paradigm for most approaches. From the other side comes the demand to develop universal concepts that, if used, will do

1. Jaroslav Pelikan, "Faith," in *The Encyclopedia of Religion,* ed. Mircea Eliade (New York: Macmillan, 1987), 5:251-52.

2. For elaboration, see Joseph J. Godfrey, S.J., "Trust the Heart of Religion: A Sketch," *American Catholic Philosophical Quarterly* 65, Annual Supplement: *Religions and the Virtue of Religion* (1991): 157-67. Godfrey quotes Raymond Panikkar, "Faith — A Constitutive Dimension of Man," *Journal of Ecumenical Studies* 8 (1971): 223-54, esp. 244-47.

most to minimize the crisis. The thesis of this book is that the development of cultures of trust will hold more promise and can draw on the energies of more citizens if there is concentration on the building blocks of a society. Those who build can then draw on both individual efforts and proposals for change on social and communal levels, including national levels and even beyond.[3]

The reach of this book, even in the scope of wild hopes and expectations, is limited to the societies that are called Western, influenced as they are by Jewish and Christian traditions as well as by classical and Enlightenment-era legacies. I will assume that we live with an ethos that I have regularly described, albeit inelegantly, as "religio-secular." In such a complex ethos, religious and nonreligious strands are woven and tangled in ever more intricate ways. Pulling at some of the strands labeled "secular" can throw light on the religious aspects of the cultural braid, and vice versa, with the "religious" informing the "secular." So I will tug at them in the next two chapters.

Advancing that task will call for efforts to retrieve half-forgotten resources, to revisit conflicts that remain half-resolved, and to discover promising connections that can strengthen cultures of trust.

---

3. The concept of "a culture of trust" is prominent in Francis Fukuyama, *Trust: The Social Virtues and the Creation of Prosperity* (New York: Simon and Schuster, 1995), pp. 33-35, an informed if controversial treatment of culture that he defines as "inherited social habit," which he then connects with "moral virtue" and "the concept of character." He poses culture as "ethical habit" over against visions of culture being based on "rational choice," which he frequently poses as the basis of productive economic orders.

The most cogent critique of Fukuyama's version of "cultures of trust" in the economic realm is Mark E. Warren, "Democratic Theory and Trust," in Warren, *Democracy and Trust* (Cambridge: Cambridge University Press, 1999), pp. 318-29. Warren cites criticism by Lynne Zucker, who says that trust may be "(1) process based . . . (2) characteristic-based . . . and (3) institutional-based." Fukuyama slights this last characteristic, a factor that makes his approach more effective in relatively static societies, where one-on-one relationships can predominate, but less so in dynamic, fluid, mobile, and less personally based societies. This means that Fukuyama uses "a premodern conception of trust," which is less useful today. "Fukuyama's faith in inherited cultural dispositions is related to the fact that he defines trust without reference to risk." He "confuses trust with something more like familiarity. . . ." Since my book is not devoted to macroeconomic concerns, we need not follow all the implications of the critiques; but we should remain aware of the limits of Fukuyama's pioneering "neo-conservative" approach.

History and Theology Addressed to a General Public: An Apologia

My approach is grounded in a decades-long experience of studying, teaching, and writing history. When I am challenged by skeptics who question my attention to trust, distrust, and mistrust as a major theme in history, I like to start with a commonsense approach. An exercise that I recommend is simple: read today's newspaper, visit the Internet, watch television, listen to the radio — all with your eyes and ears open for testimony. Tales of divorces and separations, alienation across the generations, failure of medical institutions to keep their covenants with poor patients, politicians making promises everyone knows they will break, nations paying no attention to treaties, the telling of lies — all of these have complex elements. Common to almost all of them at root are issues of trust, or its absence. So the historian in me readily responded when I was asked to isolate the theme of trust and then help resituate it in cultures of today.

A citizen, a professor, and a believer can and likely does wear more hats than one. While making a living as a professor of history, not a professional systematic theologian, I taught in a divinity school, where the import and effects of religions can be taken for granted and then scrutinized, as well as in the division of social sciences, where their weight cannot always be assumed. All the while, my third curricular forum was in the humanities, where the context was the aforementioned "Committee on the History of Culture" and where religious and secular dimensions were creatively mixed. It is this third posting that helps inspire and inform my interest in culture and cultures in this book. Given three choices from my career, in this chapter I will depend on the "divinity" connections. Since such cultures, as I have defined them, are made up of "ideas, knowledge, beliefs, norms, values, and other things," in Philip Bagby's description of "religion" and "science," I will begin partly to fill the just-constructed frame by exploring some resources in religious, philosophical, and practical ideas.

Surrealist artist René Magritte, in his Dada phase, painted a picture of a perfectly detailed smoker's pipe, under which he placed this caption: *Ceci n'est pas une pipe* ("This is not a pipe"). Some readers may suspect a parallel here, when I say that this is not a discourse in systematic theology and yet, when speaking of trust, I must at least partially approach the subject from some sort of theological angle. So, even though "this is not theology," theology enters in.

44

Allow me to elaborate on the story of background. I was invited to contribute to a project on trust at the Trust Institute of the State University of New York at Stony Brook, and I was asked to address the institute's main focus, a world in which something of what is signaled by the labels "science" and "religion" play large, often conflicting, and sometimes interactive roles. I surmised that this challenge came because I had long been identified with the theological theme of trust as it was reflected in the titles of two small books that I had edited, both of them basically anthologies of writings on trust by Martin Luther.[4] In both cases I played more the role of a master of ceremonies than a master commentator on the topic. Upon accepting the assignment at Stony Brook, I dusted off both books and checked to see what was in them that might inform my new assignment.

It was clear that, on one level at least, the approach and intention of those books differed so much from the current project that I might have been tempted to say to the Stony Brook team, "Sorry, wrong number" or "wrong address" or "mistaken identity." Perhaps an Internet search engine looking for the word "trust" put the project coordinators on my trail (though "trust" would come up a few thousand more times with reference to financial institutions than to the complex of "science and religion"). Thus the CEO of "First Bank and Trust" almost anywhere would likely be as confused as I would have been to see us in the same category, because "trust" means such very different things in those two cases.

The "bank-and-trust" approach to trust is not, of course, the only terminological alternative to its place in theology. In a pluralist society, for one other option, philosophical talk might make some meanings of the subject more immediately accessible for many. Thus the literature on trust among "the virtues" is extensive, as evidenced in readings inherited from the classical Greek and Roman writings. How philosophers spoke of virtue might seem to be more immediately relevant in our cultures than theological talk, which tends to be rooted in particular traditions and which does not lend itself easily to universalizing treatments of trust. Here, however, is where the task of retrieval from dusty theological documents begins to be relevant. It is likely that more

---

4. *The Place of Trust: Martin Luther on the Sermon on the Mount* (Minneapolis: Augsburg, 1983); *Speaking of Trust: Conversing with Luther about the Sermon on the Mount* (Minneapolis: Augsburg Fortress, 2003).

people decide what trust is and how they are to live with it from their reading of prophets like Jeremiah or the Gospel of John — or the Qur'an, for that matter — than they do from the ancient classical writings, which attract many students but not multimillion-member clusters of believers who trust such scriptural documents.

Fresh reading and research on trust, of the kind that has engaged me in recent years, has revealed that, contrary to expectations, the idea of connecting bank-and-trust "trust" with philosophical and practical "trust" in other departments of life is not so far-fetched. Some of the assumptions about human nature that undergird practices of financial organizations parallel and draw on impulses accessible in the recesses of Scripture. Steps taken to assure trust in the two cases differ, especially because security measures used to safeguard trust in the savings-and-loan world are of more stringent, visible, and perhaps efficient form than one expects to find at Sinai Temple or the Sunday school of First Presbyterian Church. Still, the two examples do complement each other and may display symbiotic relationships with each other.

Theology and Trust in Secular Settings

At once, scholars or activists in these fields become aware of the fragility of trust in human affairs. The scenes that they perceive sometimes seem to be made up of more trust-breakers than trust-keepers. Their observed world houses more card sharks and con men and women, scam artists and betrayers of public trust, cheaters on examinations and those who fail to make good on promises to repay bad debts, marital cheats and contract-breakers than it does people whose "handshake is as good as their word," their word as good as signed contracts, and their contracts recognized as genuine pledges that will be approached in confidence. Those who have read in religious and theological classics across the traditions are, or should be, unsurprised in the face of such scenes. The texts anticipate the many changes rung on themes of broken trust, and broken trust brings with it the threat of chaos or the actual arrival of chaos.

Dragging theological themes into the interdisciplinary arena on the "religio-secular" scene can be done briskly but never thoughtlessly or casually. One thinks of Reinhold Niebuhr, the towering theologian of Protestant America in the middle of the twentieth century. He was consulted by people of influence who did not share his Christian faith — "atheists for Niebuhr," some called themselves — for one stated reason: his biblically informed base for approaching the "nature and destiny" of the human drew on and displayed unmatched depth and provided resonance for interpreting humans at their worst and at their best.

It is easy to show by reference to historic expressions and their survival that theology, however defined, played and plays a part in most crucial spheres of life. Among these, for example, would be post-Orthodox and post-Soviet life in Russia, the cosmos of Jews even where they are small minorities, Scottish Presbyterianism, Islamic economies, and a multitude of cultural expressions. Most of the people who profess religion do not want to regard theology as having had life only "back there," in the antique shops and museums of cultures. Yet the historical exploration can shed fresh light on cultural and social subjects, as I hope to show here.

Paul Pribbenow, now president of Augsburg College in Minneapolis, shuttled between the School of Social Service Administration and the Divinity School for his doctoral work. Along the way he posed an interesting question about the professions that represented his fields of academic interest. Knowing that the literature produced through the centuries on the classic professions of law, religion, and medicine was vast, he focused on three twentieth-century inventions: social work, public relations, and fund-raising. Leaders in each of these were often in pursuit of some grounding in ethics and philosophy. Pribbenow inquired about which concepts that were at least once alive in the discourse about classical professions might best be translated and could be available in the transformation of these now thoroughly secular professions. He chose three concepts: vocation, mission, and stewardship.

Vocation obviously connected to the theme of trust and in many ways was the easiest for him to feature. The medieval monks were much devoted to having a vocation (*vocare*, "to call"), which they refined all their lives. Today the concept of vocation, one would admit, has itself been shifted into practical categories. So we speak of "vocational training," which ordinarily now means the acquisition of a skill to make it possible to have a job (thus there are vocational schools). Pribbenow would be reluctant to call this practical use of the concept a debasement, or to name the skills it implies unimportant. We may hope that a vocationally trained plumber or woodworker is available when needed.

But in our time the pursuit of a vocation has become rediscovered and connected with more than a career or a job. Often the shadow of religion and theology remains, since one cannot have a calling, a vocation, unless someone called, and that could be God or someone who claimed to be a representative of God. Those who sense a vocation to help build cultures of trust within our society may consider theirs to be a somehow divine call, and others will ground their response in frankly humanistic bids. Needless to say, being aware of one's vocation will have a bearing on conceptions and practices of trusting.

A second category that Pribbenow thought could help inform people in the new professions was *mission,* which also obviously connects with the theme of trust. Just as vocation implies a caller, mission depends on a sender (*missio,* "to send"), and that could be God or those who claim to be God's agents. "Mission" simply became the name for a task to be carried out: for example, one sees it used in the locutions of military engagement. In the larger sense it informs complex assignments. For a couple of centuries, but more explicitly in recent times, citizens have spoken of America as "having a mission." Industries and corporations favor "mission statements." These are sometimes merely formal, not noticed by any but the executives who had their firm pay for an advertisable mantra. Yet, as with "vocation," the use of the term "mission" prompts some valuable questions about the authorizer of mission, and the varied answers to the question can contribute to reflection and revised action. Again, some will consider the development of cultures of trust to be part of a divinely mandated mission, while others will pursue it on other grounds, though these will have a reminiscence to the one grounded in what is perceived as a sacred impetus.

A third theme, *stewardship,* like the other two, is easily associated with the category of trust. It remains a somewhat more church-protected term, one that is put to work by synagogues and churches when they want to raise money — or change lives. They cite stewardship — in the Christian case, with backing in the parables and examples of Jesus — to show how through human planning a provident God acts among serious people, often to good material effect and certainly for spiritual strengthening. The idea of working, saving, investing, and being generous has been so attractive and effective in the churches that its meanings could not be quarantined in sanctuary settings during sacred speaking and acts.

In Pribbenow's observation and testing, companies whose members learned stewardship, whether they believed in a divine Steward or not, did better than those where the ethos was "easy-come, easy-go" with respect to money. Today people speak of stewarding the natural resources of the globe, for which they set up environment-friendly causes and often see themselves as divinely mandated to be stewards, while others explicitly use no such grounds. Yet the biblical (or other religious) resources and impetuses behind stewardship remain to inform it.

In this kind of setting, I now propose to add "trust," observed as a malleable, multipurpose concept that can carry over some of its theological cachet or connotations and make contributions partly independent of a theological source. Like cultures in which trust plays a part — vocation, mission, and stewardship — it can come to prominence and will be basic in what we are calling cultures of trust. To propose such trust is useful in contemporary and often secular analogies. This means that one must probe what it has meant when writers of sacred scriptures or pastoral manuals took it up, revised it, or partly ran away from it, awed as they were by its potential. In a society in which more than 80 percent of the citizens have some knowledge of, attachment to, and, potentially, curiosity about religious interests in trust, it will deserve more exploration than we can give it, but we can begin by pointing in promising directions.

Analogies Among Transcendent and Immanent Claims

An important point implied in the preceding paragraph is this: connecting trust in the divine with human trust can only be done by analogy. In this context I would define analogy along these lines: when bringing two assertions into comparison as being analogical, we note that within every similarity there is a difference and in every difference there may be a similarity. The most familiar illustration is the classic analogy between sleep and death. In a person's sleep there are parallels to death: in both cases the same person, the same body is involved; in both cases the agent has no consciousness and is not participating in any acts that live people do (except, we note, to "lie there"). The big difference is that one wakes in the case of sleep and does not in the case of death. That is a sufficiently drastic difference, one that ought to lead anyone from the brink of temptation to see "sameness." At the same time, there is enough "likeness" to inspire metaphorical, or what I would call "mirror," usages. Thus hymnody and poetry about death often point to the person as "sleeping," having entered the sphere of "eternal rest." No, she's *dead*.

So, when we make a study of biblical and theological uses of trust, we shall have two elements in mind. First is trust in God, and, sometimes and in special contexts, God's trust in humans. Whoever observes or counsels developing it knows that trust in the divine is qualitatively different from human-to-human trust. But, second, when we use the mirror of divine trust on the human scene, some similarities, metaphors, examples, and mandates for consequent action can inform human trust.

The great breakdown that strains analogy but assures the difference among the similarities is that biblical concepts of trust in connection with faith always center in God for believers: God alone can be trusted absolutely. Removing God from the discourse alters it completely. I recall the wedding of two graduate students who asked a theologian friend to perform their marriage. Being their friend, he agreed to do so, but they had a singular request of the theologian: they did not want him to mention the name of God or make any reference to a transcendent deity. Their theologian friend courteously went through the motions as if he were a justice of the peace. When the wedding was over, he asked my wife and me to drive him home, and on the way he mused: "There were rings and flowers and songs and liturgical-sounding phrases and readings and photographs, but it all reminded me of a large gleaming Cadillac, ready to go — except that its motor had been removed."

In this book, trust will seldom refer to trust in God except to frame analogy, since our interest is in human cultural affairs. That does not mean that we shall break away with the chassis of a Cadillac but no motor. With that in mind, we turn to at least selective and rudimentary features of biblical witness to trust.

In the West: A Focus on Biblical Trust

The use of the term "biblical" here might sound as if we are to picture a simple, coherent, unified subject called trust within a scriptural canon. However, the Bible is not a single-authored argument but a complex, sometimes contradictory collection by many authors who exemplified their place in different circumstances and demonstrated diverse attitudes, moods, and responses. Rather than bewail that feature, many believers celebrate it, since an awareness of that feature offers more amplitude and variety, and it protects nonfundamentalists from turning that complex "library" into a simple and always coherent textbook, rulebook, or book of codes. It also means that some of the analogies lead to lessons one must unlearn or repudiate, given efforts by so many to impose one set of meanings on the whole book, the "library."

Finally, if the analogy works in the sense that the example throws light on human affairs, there must at least be some possibility that those who would not classify themselves as believers in the witness of the Bible might draw on it as they might draw on Plato without being Platonists or Maimonides if they are not Jews or Confucius if they are not Confucianists.

Fair warning: to introduce a classic text and especially a text seen as sacred will not lead to any safe and clear-cut path to the ways of trust. Indeed, most of such texts and most assuredly Hebrew Scripture and the New Testament, privileged for centuries in Western cultures, do not begin by setting forth trust as some easy-to-gain dimension of human life. Whoever might use a concordance or search engine to track down the many uses of the category of trust in such scriptures would be jolted with a dose of realism. The realism is so prominent that one could plausibly consider that the book cherished as the Bible is mainly a textbook of examples and cautions about the *risk* of trusting.

For this act of condensed reference, I will draw informally on a short entry by the British commentator Donald Guthrie in his *New Testament Theology,* but I will reconfigure and paraphrase his statements for present purposes.[5] When discussing science, religion, and public discourse, I shall concentrate on the role communication plays in trust and distrusting. If one does not hear, mishears, or distorts what he hears, it is difficult to respond with trust.

1. For our discourse on discourse or conversation on conversation, the most dramatic biblical theme is an emphasis on the role of *speaking and hearing* (or conversing) in the developing of trust. This would be the case in both individual and social applications, always on the divine-human model. In the initiating and climactic words of the writer Paul

5. Donald Guthrie, *New Testament Theology* (Downers Grove, IL: InterVarsity, 1981), pp. 591-94.

in his New Testament letters, references to God portray God as being faithful, giving assurances that God is reliable (1 Thess. 5:24): "He who calls you is faithful, and he will do it."

More frequently, faith *(pistis)* refers to the human trust in God. Relevant again to our subsequent discussions of how trust is transacted through conversation — that is, speaking and hearing — are the texts that point to a connection through hearing someone who is trustworthy. "Hearing" is the activity that is associated with human invitations to trust. Conversation, pledging, and taking oaths normally have an auditory dimension. One says, "I'll believe that, if she comes here, looks me in the eye, and says it!" In biblical witness, the beckoner leaves a visible sign for ambiguous empirical tests less frequently than bids through the voice. The God of the Bible is one who speaks, and even creates cosmos out of chaos on page one by speaking. One reveals through utterance, the other hears and makes a decision, often a drastic choice.[6] Such a response is not a fully finished product, because trust demands and deserves constant nurture and development. This is another instance where the analogy works: if assurances of trust are figuratively locked in a spiritual safety deposit box, little happens. Constant or frequent interactions based on the sense of developing assurance is what matters. Cultures of trust progress through some form or other of conversation.

Those who live in a culture where majorities respond to a God who speaks but do not themselves respond to God, or consider any claims for God credible, cannot escape dealing with people who do. They have enormous power in voting, supporting or blocking legislation, setting hospital policies, inspiring volunteer work, and offering or denying signs of trust themselves.

2. In such biblical exchanges, the faith that is initiated by hearing gets developed when emotional and character-shaping factors come into play. Thus trust inspires *boldness and risk,* because risk is integral to all talk about trust. When someone extends and invests in trust, the other (the respondent) is asked to abandon the tentativeness she brought to the potential transaction. Various Greek words suggest that the trusted and trusting person expresses the new situation with "boldness." When a leader is confident, he can show confidence in others who have had a similar engendering experience: "I have great confidence in you" (2 Cor. 7:4). Paul thus speaks not only of confidence but of

6. Guthrie, *New Testament Theology,* pp. 591-94.

52

"great" confidence, and not because he and his readers are physically near each other, where they could count on each other's presence and power. Instead, what has occurred is a certifying experience on which the writer can draw. Boldness is, of course, only one aspect of the expression of trust in another person who first does the emboldening. In Hebrew Scripture the root usage comes with the verb *Hiph'il,* to "trust" something or someone because a relationship exists, and such a relationship inspires boldness. Cultures of trust involve people who are ready for risks boldly taken.

3. Sometimes biblical usages move the concept of trust into *the zone of confidence.* One can have confidence that a bank will safely protect funds or that the elevator one is riding on will not (ordinarily!) fail. Faith in Hebrew Scripture, however, refers less to "trust that" than to "trust in." Secondarily, it carries over to the idea of trusting in what is associated with a personal God. Words like "solid" and "firm" and "being true" are associated with the Hebrew word for trusting, and they carry a force that allows for a person to be worthy of trust, to inspire confidence. There are many biblical references to trust in a person or persons. To trust is to have confidence in persons or things, usually because a pledge or guarantee has already been given.

The concept of trust glides easily from association with verbs and nouns to adjectives. In a way, this illustrates a contention that the certification of trust occurs as experiences that depict embodiments of trust and exemplarity on the part of one who bids for trust. On occasion, though believers could never see God — this was always made clear — they could gain trust by observing a fellow believer, such as Abraham, Samuel, or David. Thus, in the Greek version of the Septuagint text, Abraham is called "the faithful one," the recipient and imparter of trust (Num. 12:7), as in the book of Galatians. The believer can carry over trust to impersonal things that are believed to have divine authorization, such as commandments (Ps. 110:7) or covenants (Ps. 88). Here, as elsewhere, the reach of faith extends to the imparter of the covenant. Yahweh made a covenant and expected — even demanded — a response (Deut. 7:6-7). The cultures of trust, by analogy to the divine, depend on the faith and faithfulness, the pledges and promises, of humans.

4. Our interest in building cultures of trust is met by biblical discussions of some *communal aspects.* Often neglected, even by many who confess faith in scriptural revelations and commandments, is the fact that trust and trustworthiness are most often expressions not of isolated

individuals but of the community. Those who were invited into the sphere of believers learn to trust there, and then to advance trust among those in or attracted to the community. Consequently, the fate of trust-relations depends in no small measure on the health of that community. A note to file away for later discussions of communities of trust is the biblical observation that broken trust in smaller parts of the gatherings infects or jeopardizes more, even the whole gathering of people. It is true that in many psalms an individual responds to the divine invitation, but the normal responses are communal. By now it should be obvious that, in my observation and argument, along with my interest in constructing cultures of trust, trusting is not the isolated act of an individual; rather, it depends on interaction with others who are open to trust.

5. Having noticed that "faith comes by hearing" more than by seeing or receiving signs, it is true that on occasion "trust talk" includes the *giving and receiving of signs.* Frankly, and at first glance at least, this is one of the more difficult features of biblical talk about trust to apply, even by analogy, in the modern world. A person sometimes trusted Yahweh in part because of signs Yahweh gave. Since a sign is the mark of the presence of God, its absence when it would have mattered was troubling. These signs that did inspire risk and communal action were most familiar in the stories associated with the divine call to flee slavery in Egypt; but they also appear at other moments of challenge and trouble (Isa. 7:10-17). Since these are connected with what most moderns, including many believers, would see as miraculous or supernatural interruptions, we would be led into mythic paths and pasts if these were to be explored for analogy. However, whoever reads popular accounts of deliverances or healings will often hear or read of survivors pointing to specific signs of response in prayer. Since the interest here is not in literal applications but in the use of analogy, we can leave the scene of the signs unresolved.

6. Some may question whether, even by analogy, another dimension of witness in Hebrew Scripture has to be understood by those who would build communities of trust: fear. The *fear of Yahweh* that exists in the lives of people lives on by analogy in the experience of awe associated with profound acts of trust. Soldiers speak of this as they enter battle, no matter how confident they were in their weaponry or their comrades. When life-and-death matters are integral to an experience of trust or being suspicious, all alert and sensitive people will know something of awe. Moses was asked to take the shoes off his feet, for the

ground on which he was standing was holy ground. Job was stunned in the face of the Presence on whom he depended. The believers within Israel exemplified the fear of God despite or within or because of their confidence and trust. In a kind of stick-and-carrot approach, the threat that induced fear was never isolated or disconnected from the mercy, grace, and love of God. In the Psalms we see instances where deeper trust in a more profound "other" helped free someone from lesser naggings and hassling. The one who fears Yahweh, the source who beckons others to experience awe, was to be freed from lesser givers of imperatives. Job 4:6 presents remarkable questions by a friend of the sufferer: "Is not your fear of God your confidence?" This confidence again calls for the sorting of the credentials and commitments associated with trust-giving. Absolute faith in Yahweh relativized and often ruled out other kinds of faith. The turn that the responder makes can be translated to mean that, God aside, we should be wary of absolutes. As one of my teachers advised, in counsel that applies here: we are to take something "very, very seriously, but not too seriously." An exclusive note enters here: the respondent in faith and trust is convinced that nothing about trust applies to the idols, images, and deities that surrounded the faithful.

In the writings of Judaism that survive from two centuries before and one century into the Common Era, many of the Hebrew scriptural themes are still to be found, though one can recognize that, reflected in them, an ever more complex view of trust in Jewish ordinances and practices receives emphasis. The texts enjoin a vigorous distancing from those of surrounding faith communities. In these contexts again, scholars note increasing emphasis on "belief that" more than on "belief in." The greatest scholar of the period, Philo (20 BCE to 49 CE), posed a greater distance between trust in God and trust in earthly things. At the same time, rabbinical Judaism was devoted to the more traditional pattern of confidence in the covenant and the commandments — and the giver of both, Yahweh. The rabbis also associated trust with trustworthiness among the people of the covenant, along with exemplary devotion to the will of God. There, as elsewhere, believers were to follow the example of the pioneer risk-taker, Abraham, who trusted God and whom people could emulate.

7. Of less interest than these but still applicable by analogy to human-to-human trust-relations are evidences that appear in somewhat later early Christian writings. As a base for human trusting, faith

as trust in God began to give way to *faith as assent* to certain tenets, propositions, or dogmas. Thereupon, if we are to take the Jesus texts as the main guides, it is clear that believers in churches who could speak of professing "articles of faith," valuable as they may be in other contexts, find them to be secondary. In the Gospels, Jesus presented more of what we would call "articles of trust." The movement within the New Testament writings reflects the development of the community of believers, and it reveals more and more interest in seeing faith directed to doctrines. These and other instruments helped provide borders to the community, but they are of less interest here. In cultures of trust there will inevitably be some boundaries and borders, but they may be porous, more devoted to interpersonal involvements than enforcing of codes. The long pull of religious history, however, shows that policies of exclusion and segregation often tend to take over.

The Character of Humans and Its Complications for Trust

Occasionally, biblical writings will celebrate loyalty among humans, a signal that such persons could trust each other and be trustworthy. Such affirmations run counter to the contentions about the character and action of humans in many of the biblical books. The authors may claim that humans are made in the image of God, but all the writers who get near the subject agree that something has happened to humans that makes them more inclined to be untrustworthy than trustworthy. Humans, even the best of them, turn out to be bad risks. All the reasons given for people to have confidence in God are reversed or flipped over, so the expectations will instead lead to a lack of confidence and a need to address the problems that come from the absence of trust among humans.

The classic statement of the occasion for this change has been named "the Fall of man" (the concept of "man" still served inclusively, i.e., for all humans). Biblical literalists, who number in the many millions, relate this accounting of a fall to a narrative in the book of Genesis. Adam and Eve disobeyed God, so all humans issuing from them — which, to those literalists, means all humans — have also "fallen." Christians who might like to dismiss the concept as being restricted to Hebrew Scripture cannot lightly dismiss the fact that in the New Testament, in his letter to the Romans, the apostle Paul picks up on the Genesis narrative and connects all humans with one, Adam, just as he re-lates all the saved with one, Jesus Christ.

In those Scripture passages, humans were originally to be seen as trustworthy because they had been created in and for perfection. But they had been given free choice, and they chose to disobey God. The de-tails of the story, so rich in theological implications and so bewildering or offensive to those who reject the mythical elements of the biblical story, are sufficiently removed from normal expectations about human nature that all but literalists would find them off-putting if not bizarre. It is difficult for them to picture basing views of trust and mistrust on vi-sions of human nature after the Fall. For the past two centuries, after the rise of the "historical-critical" approach to works such as Genesis and attempts to "demythologize" the faith, the story of eating forbid-den fruit and seduction by a snake are no part of their faithful under-standing. Such believers shelve these along with cartoon depictions and endless jokes. Yet, the more critical and "unmythical" the interpre-tations of moderns have become, many believers charge that the theme of the Fall of man is matched by not *un*mythical but by *other*-mythical interpretations from modern times.

In the Christian vocabulary — though, remarkably, not in the Jewish one — the trust-breaking consequence of the Fall is "original sin," by whatever name it lives on. In many of the Christian traditions where this phrase appears, claims about it are based not only on ontology (in the nature of "being itself") or on Scripture (on how things are revealed to be) but on observation. One reviewer of the work of Reinhold Niebuhr observed that this "original sin" was "the only empirically verifiable Christian doctrine." Those who agreed with Niebuhr's position noted that you could observe the consequences of original sin in human ac-tion, which was often destructive of trust, whether from the viewpoint of what God demanded or what humans needed and expected. Applying the term in a culture that cannot easily comprehend what it was in-tended to signal can introduce as much confusion as it might offer clar-ity in our context. One need go no further than to cite Catholic theolo-gian Karl Rahner, who speaks of the gap between perfection and reality as a statement that points to the "state of what ought not to be."[7]

---

7. Quoted by Mary Ann Hinsdale, "Infinite Openness to the Infinite: Karl Rahner's Contribution to Modern Catholic Thought on the Child," in *The Child in Christian Thought*, ed. Marcia J. Bunge (Grand Rapids: Eerdmans, 2001), 429-30.

The understanding of the human in the image of God implied in such contexts survives (Gen. 9:6), but the negative side has taken over, and we find now a dialectic of human good and evil that informs all talk about trust and nontrust. Some medieval theologians came up with a memorable if too clever condensation in Latin. It downgrades all claims of natural human dependability: the human who once had not been able to sin *(posse non peccare)* now couldn't *not* sin *(non posse non peccare)*. Jews did not follow this interpretive trail, so in Orthodox Judaism one hears that Adam's fall affected only Adam. Liberal Christians will have nothing to do with these literal details, but often find and offer no "higher" view than do literalists of human nature as it affects untrustworthiness. Both liberals and literalists, as Christians, counter the human flaw by relating Jesus Christ to the "new creation." Within this interpretation, God sees naturally stained humans as living within a new reality and with new potential. They are, however, no more likely to throw away locks and keys or instruments of personal or national security than are the literalists.

What of the possibility that the development of trust could lead eventually to the development of perfect reliability? In most versions of Christian theology, the human was created in perfection, to be perfect, and to be perfected. Some religious scholars have spoken of the background to all this as "original innocence." If this were how humans were and are to be encountered in history, trust would not be necessary. No one would be a threat to anyone else, and all would offer the good to all others. Yet in the biblical traditions one encounters humans mainly in their imperfection. Any talk of no-risk and of the possibility of complete trustworthiness in others would demand such radical redefinition that it is of no use in our context. Here one thinks of Wesleyan and other Christian teachers of perfection and their heirs, who also keep locks on their doors and certify pledges with personal signatures, including with their fellow believers. Or one must argue, as some Christians have, that perfect trustworthiness is eschatological, which means that it comes after or beyond the historical existence of the individual. Again, short of that end point, one needs locks and vows and signatures — all of them signals of the compromising of trust.

Making the Best of the Circumstances

Humans as they are encountered in history, then, are not "naturally" to be trusted and are wary when they extend trust to other humans. Emphasizing human innocence and perfection means that, in our case, all evidences of the absence of trust and trustworthiness can issue in defeatism or fatalism. There has been a fall, and nothing much can be done about it. However, in most interpretations, biblical witness does not end in tragedy and hopelessness, which would mean the removal of all bases for trust. If one begins with the observation of a fallen world, it is more immediately appropriate to ask what is to be made of the mix of good building materials and debris. The creative agents throughout history found their own reasons for refusing to be morally paralyzed or defeated. Christians have their own particular accounts and definitions and strategies for good living in spite of this original sin, even if this means that one cannot offer, expect, or realize perfection and assure trust-relations. They also remind others: "Your eyes do not simply deceive: you observe, at least on rare occasions, the fact that some people turn responsible, become objects of trust, are trustworthy, and extend trust to others." How this positive relationship to trust occurs, given a beginning among things not being as "they ought to be," helps inspire strategies for dealing with broken trust and calls for moving beyond half-repaired situations of trust.

Significantly, Jesus, the central Christian figure, the one who speaks so often about untrustworthiness and sin, is never cited as mentioning original sin, the Fall, or Adam in his discourses. In the Fourth Gospel there is a glimpse of his followers' grasp of his understanding. Early in that text Jesus was seen in Jerusalem for the Passover festival, where many saw the "signs" that he was performing, so they followed him. Should not their favor have led him to put confidence in them? The text is specific about his "no!" and the reasons for it. "But Jesus on his part would not entrust himself to them, because he knew all people and needed no one to testify about anyone; for he himself knew what was in everyone" (John 2:24-25).

Often cited as a condensation of prophetic views concerning mistrust is a fervent verse from the eighth-century BCE prophet Micah, usually seen as a witness to the steadfast love of a compassionate God, one who set forth something gentle, a kind of sign that God worked through human agency:

He has told you, O mortal, what is good;
and what does the Lord require of you
but to do justice, and to love kindness,
and to walk humbly with your God? (Mic. 6:8)

But Micah follows this with a call to suspicion, not only of strangers and neighbors, but even of one's best friend, family member, or lover:

Put no trust in a friend,
Have no confidence in a loved one;
Guard the doors of your mouth
from her who lies in your embrace.
For the son treats the father with contempt,
the daughter rises up against her mother,
the daughter-in-law against her mother-in-law;
your enemies are members of your own household. (Mic. 7:5-6)

This is followed by a characteristic turn in the prophets, from untrustworthy humans to God as trustworthy and the giver of trust:

But as for me, I will look to the Lord,
I will wait for the God of my salvation;
my God will hear me. (Mic. 7:7)

If one is to be cautious about trusting even friends, certainly the enemy will elicit nothing but suspicion. And if the lowly sometimes connive to break trust, the stakes are raised when it comes to the mighty. One reason not to confide in those of higher status is that the protection they can give is always temporary and limited.

A classic verse often overlooked by those who serve authority uncritically and beckon others to do the same is Psalm 146:3-4:

Do not put your trust in princes, in mortals, in whom there is
   no help.
When their breath departs, they return to the earth;
on that very day their plans perish.

Not only the mortality of the powerful raises caution about trusting them. The Prophets and the Gospels regularly show that the accumulation of power leads to a loss of perspective and an exertion of power at the expense of others. Rather than scan the whole of Scripture for statements like these, suffice it to say that the views of human potential and limits from author to author, from book to book, is consistent. Only God is to be trusted, even if one cannot know the divine mind and mysteries. It is humans that are on the spot, demanding and deserving alertness on the part of their friends or enemies to be mistrustful of all people. We cannot build cultures of trust on the basis of faith in the natural trustworthiness of humans.

In biblical settings, one did not need to be specially called by God, as the prophets claimed to be, or to be poetically gifted, as the psalmists show they were, to know something of "what is in everyone" and thus to limit the occasions and depth of the bonds of trust. The issue has always been this: given such observations or ideologically defended contentions about the propensity of people to be untrustworthy, what can anyone do about it? Be stunned and paralyzed? Make up counterstories, which might inspire counteractions?

To know what was in the human, each human, as Jesus knew, according to the writers of the Gospels, did not turn up bright pictures for optimists. If one came to be "in Christ," Paul argued, he or she became a "new creature" and was then capable of carrying on the life of God among people. Yet such a person did not leave behind the disposition to do evil, and all did evil. For that reason, biblical writers posed people between the images of perfection, that is, of the human in the image of God, *and* the same human — even at the same time — becoming a suspect, someone to mistrust. A quick canvass of biblical utterances and observations makes this clear.

An Interpretation of Interpretation: A Hermeneutics of Trust

Most religious texts, including those in Hebrew Scripture and the New Testament, do not abandon people to the devices that come with their suspicions, records of distrust, and statements that sound pessimistic about the human condition. Instead, through the ages people have used these texts to inspire trust. Richard B. Hays, a scholar at Duke Divinity School and author of *The Moral Vision of the New Testament*, advocates the suspicion of suspicion. He was invited to put the question of trusting texts before a readership that was attuned to the debate about suspicion. He calls his essay "Salvation by Trust? Reading the Bible Faithfully."

In putting this question forward, Hays moves the subject before us to the center of interpretive concerns. He first refers to the sixteenth-century Reformers who helped produce Protestantism, which he sees to be a cluster of interpretive biblical schools. This reference draws attention to the gap between the assumptions of those Reformers and anyone studying Scripture today. "Living as we do on this side of the Enlightenment, we cannot escape the intellectual impact of the great 'masters of suspicion': Nietzsche, Freud, Marx and more recently Foucault, along with other purveyors of 'critical theory.'" They set out to demystify language and expose "the ways in which our linguistic and cultural systems are constructed by ideologies that further the interests of those who hold power."[8] Do not trust anyone in power — that's the inclusive message.

Of course, the Bible has been the most attractive and threatened object of such suspicious study. Citizens may care greatly about the novels of Dickens, but such literature is not in any measure large enough to shape a culture. The Bible is. Hays adduces the work of Elisabeth Schüssler Fiorenza, whose field is feminist interpretation.[9] Hays reads her as placing a warning label on biblical texts, a call to mistrust: *Caution! Could be dangerous to your health and survival!* She and her cohort do not reject the Bible, and most of them find liberating texts within it. But Fiorenza's ideological critique discovers and reproduces biblical texts that sanction and even command violence "against women, children and the powerless." Hays follows these critics a long way, to the point at which he asks, If the Bible is such an agent of oppression, how could anyone trust it or see it as liberating anyone? He does not follow Schüssler Fiorenza as far as adopting her "feminist critical hermeneutic" as an alternative. It depends not on the Bible but on "women's own experience and vision of liberation," which she treats unambiguously. He treats it ambiguously, first paying respect to the interpretive approach and then raising serious questions.

Hays argues that the hermeneutics of suspicion is to be balanced, or countered, by an often overlooked (at least in scholarly circles) alter-

---

8. Richard B. Hays, "Salvation by Trust? Reading the Bible Faithfully," *Christian Century,* Feb. 26, 1997, p. 218.

9. The discussion of Schüssler-Fiorenza follows. Hays, "Salvation by Trust?" pp. 218-23.

native, something that is both necessary and primary, which he calls "a hermeneutics of trust." Hays the New Testament scholar shows how Paul the apostle, in the Epistle to the Romans, taught those open to being taught how to "suspect our own suspicions," which draws Hays to a dialectic of faith and unfaith. Applied to his fellow Jews, who make up Israel and its descendants, the apostle and letter-writer Paul saw unfaith, *apistia,* to be located in Israel's failure to obey God's Torah and "to trust God's covenant promises." Not trusting the word of God in their own scriptures, they had drifted into suspicion and unfaithfulness. How he details this drift or departure in Romans 9–11 need not concern us here, but it is important to notice how Paul celebrates the patriarch whom Jews and Christians consider the father of faith, Abraham. The promise that he and his equally aged wife Sarah were to have children was not believable, Martin Luther noted, but still Abraham believed. "No *apistia* made him waver concerning the promise of God, but he grew strong in trust *(pistis)* as he gave glory to God, being fully convinced that God was able to do what he had promised" (Rom. 4:21).

This trust went *against* aged Abraham's experience and should have elicited a hermeneutic of suspicion toward the divine word. Yet he wrestled with his doubts, discounted his own experience, "rejected skepticism, and clung to the promise of God." Thus Abraham became "the prototype of the community of faith . . . [and] exemplifies a hermeneutic of consent, a hermeneutic of trust." Hays likes the phrase about "consent" so much that he proposes it as an entry into the hermeneutics debates. For Paul, the effort by humans to adopt this alternative hermeneutics is not to be chalked up to Abraham as his good deed of the day, but was rather exemplary of the generosity of God, who made and keeps promises. Paul was troubled at first by his own conclusion and spent three chapters, Romans 9–11, illustrating the hermeneutics of trust.

Hays has to pose this question: "If we adopt a hermeneutics of trust, what becomes of the hermeneutics of suspicion? Is all questioning to be excluded, all critical reading banished?" His answer is Pauline: "By no means." Readers of Scripture with the hermeneutics of trust in God in mind "discover that we should indeed be suspicious — suspicious first of ourselves. . . ." Paul himself never stopped being suspicious of himself. Still, through all the storms within him and without, he became an agent of trust whose writing has inspired believers through the centuries and provided definitions for those who are not believers but who also are engaged in promoting cultures of trust.

CHAPTER 4

Humanistic Reflections

— ⊸⟨◉⟩⊶ —

We live in scripted societies. National constitutions, party platforms, creedal traditions, cultic codes, ancient epics, and even countercultural manifestoes provide scripts for those who would build cultures of trust and determine who is trustworthy, and show why trust is so often broken. In North American society, for those who believe and would follow biblical messages and norms, sacred scriptures play a foundational part, however compromised they may be by their believers or resisted by nonbelievers. In public discourse, statecraft, academic life, mass media, and markets, other resources are more conventionally recognized. We think of them as accessibly humanistic.

What "Humanistic" Means Here

The term "humanism" needs definition. To some, "humanism" comes only with the adjective "secular"; they picture it as something that rules out reference to the divine. In this discussion I place the accent on the humanism of the humanities: philosophy, history, linguistics, religious studies, and the like. The Commission on the Humanities (on p. 1 of its report in 1980) did not define humanities so much as it described their traditions and roles in both serviceable and provocative ways:

> [T]he humanities mirror our own image and our image of the world. Through the humanities we reflect on the fundamental question:

what does it mean to be human? The humanities offer clues but never a complete answer. They reveal how people have tried to make moral, spiritual, and intellectual sense of a world in which irrationality, despair, loneliness, and death are as conspicuous as birth, friendship, hope, and reason. We learn how individuals or societies define the moral life and try to attain it, attempt to reconcile freedom and the responsibilities of citizenship, and express themselves artistically. The humanities do not necessarily mean humanness, nor do they always inspire the individual with what Cicero called "incentives to noble action." But by awakening a sense of what it might be like to be someone else or to live in another time or culture, they tell us about ourselves, stretch our imagination, and enrich our experience. They increase our distinctively human potential.[1]

Every line and phrase in that description has a bearing on trust. The whole text points to resources on which those who would build and maintain cultures of trust can draw. In modern, pluralist societies, those that are often called secular, the limits of resorting to sacred texts will be at least as obvious as are the assets. A problem of religious communities — but not of them alone, by any means — is obvious when they generate enclaves exclusive to those who belong to each. Those in them often fail to seek or find reasons for trusting those who are not belongers. People within such circles tend to find texts of groups other than their own to be irrelevant, incomprehensible, or even repellent.

In the face of such barriers, the first counsel is to put religious ideas on the back shelves because they imply that favor was shown to specific chosen people, who claim privileged divine revelation offered them, or who are taught to produce negative reactions to others. It is easier, if you are a Jew or an evangelical, to dismiss a Buddhist, a Mennonite, or a Unitarian. Of course, anyone who thinks that religious groupings alone are exclusivist or sectarian has never attended a convention of anthropologists, philosophers, or academics of any discipline, who also often divide themselves into defined schools remote from or hostile to others.

Secular philosophies, for all the aspirations of some of them, do not serve universally as bases. Only philosophy majors at universities or

---

1. *The Humanities in American Life* (Berkeley: University of California Press, 1980), p. 1. The authorship is listed as "Report on the Commission on the Humanities"; I remember, in particular, the significant role of Gaines Post, Jr.

members of "Great Books" reading groups are likely to be familiar with most writings on trust found in humanistic cultures. Such students would be hidden from view and their interests would be found to be unrepresentative of what attracts most other races, ethnic groups, religious communities, and social classes. For one example, in practicing trust or bewailing those who fail to keep it, most Native Americans would not be likely to recognize the texts of Isaiah *or* Plato. Instead, often satisfactory transactions among Sioux or Zuni or Cherokee peoples draw on what are still called "tribal" stories. They are not in sacred scriptures or Great Books; rather, they were passed on orally and remain influential even in the centuries after these once-oral cultures have become literate. Similarly, as for trust among societies that represent immigrations from Southeast Asia after the Vietnam War, those who would do business, provide counseling, listen to stories, or discern folkways will find themselves tracing their way among Cambodian, Thai, Hmong, and other traditions and ways of life. The impulses to develop, measure, improve, and enjoy cultures of trust in a global and pluralist society are unimaginably diverse. Whoever explores them will find that many offer promises that compete with the offerings of others.

Sources in Classical and Enlightenment Philosophies

Having said that, however, just as we turned to Jewish and Christian biblical influences on the religious ground floor of Western society, so we can look at some classical sources and then at several more modern philosophers who have commented on trust ("classical sources" means especially ancient Greek philosophy). Alfred North Whitehead commented that Western philosophy is a series of footnotes to Plato. Hyperbolic though that may be, one cannot go far into the history of Christian doctrine, political thought, or moral and ethical discourse without finding the shadow of Plato or the light brought by Platonic thought involved with them. Many of us would have to supplement, complement, or counter Whitehead by noting that what he said of Plato's influence could also be said of Aristotle. Catholic doctrine, many assumptions in science, and statements in statecraft are footnotes to and elaborations of Aristotle's writings, so he also is regularly cited, and much of what he says informs examinations of trust to our day. It is a text by Plato, however, that is most frequently quoted when talk of trust and its limits, the trusted and their motives, comes into the conversation. Many centuries later, when philosophers again debated trust, this time in "post-Christendom," when sacred scriptures were no longer imposed on whole societies, "footnotes to Plato" appeared.

Prominent among the Enlightenment-era thinkers, such as David Hume, John Locke, and Jean-Jacques Rousseau, was Thomas Hobbes, whose view of human nature made everyone appear to be naturally untrustworthy and in need of structures that would make something that looked like trust available. Citizens who have never read a page of these thinkers — or have never even heard of them — live under their influence. Most of the Enlightenment thinkers (Rousseau being a rare exception) and their successors concentrated on depicting humans trusting and being trustworthy. But these are not the normal or normative expressions of the human condition. The records of history and their own experiences taught them that mistrust and distrust come more naturally, and societies have to devise ways to take over the roles of trust. This means contracts, covenants, and constitutions that have policing and punitive powers, which most of us take for granted in everyday life.

In societies where people can afford security, the nearly universal presence of locks on doors, safety deposit boxes, the bonding of people who have fiduciary responsibility, the notarizing of contracts, the exacting of vows when people take public office or marry, and the insistence on oaths send out signals: oaths and contracts are of particular importance because they put in oral or written words binding pledges and make or imply threats to those who break those pledges. All these measures demonstrate what is obvious on commonsense terms: societies have to take precautions against the potential disturbing or evil acts of others. They have to make strenuous efforts to assure that something like trust has a chance. Developing cultures and subcultures of trust reduces the need for so many restrictive and punitive measures, and thus their presence can be seen as economical in the larger society.

These philosophical traditions from Plato through Hobbes did not need a doctrine of the Fall or of original sin. Still, almost all of them have to begin with realistic appraisals of the human nature that they have observed and experienced all around them, and, of course, among and within them. Only some hopeful visionaries among them then offered prescriptions for some ideas and structures that encourage trust and prod citizens to become trustworthy. Few of these Western philosophers, though they have lived in often biblically scripted societies, would locate the origin or presence of human limits in an event or story, such as one about a Garden of Eden or a religious tradition of stories. They might use empirical means such as opening their eyes and ears to signals around them as they formulated their views of human basics; however they came to these, though, for most of them the picture of the natural human was no cheerier than were those of the elaborators on the theme of original sin.

Perhaps I have sped too rapidly past a noting of exceptions to the claims of those who begin with realistic views of human nature. They deserve more notice. Some were idealists and others utopians, but they worked on the common basis of positive and optimistic assumptions about human nature. To them, people are just naturally good. *Society,* in their eyes, may for various reasons be corrupted and corrupting; but individuals have it in them to be naturally trusting and trustworthy. Even in our own time — perhaps especially in our own time — in the midst of mountainous records of broken trust, we still find versions of these philosophies in popular and prosperous seminars and best-selling books devoted to self-improvement and societal fulfillment. Huge publishing industries are based on the assumption that, with some guidance and with the removal of many human-made barriers, the natural trustworthiness of people can emerge, will dominate, and all will be well.

Beginning with the predominating alternative, the realistic set of assumptions has not meant that the realists must be blinded by pessimism or need condemn themselves to indifference, paralysis, or nihilism. Instead, creative and positive suggestions in the face of human limits can produce and often have produced some positive results. An example of these is apparent in the world of interreligious dialogue and intercultural conversation, which have addressed and overcome some kinds of misunderstanding and conflict. If intellectual mistrust is born because antagonists live in two different mental worlds — picture those of "science" and "religion" — some philosophers can help guide them to approaches that will not lead to instant and full agreement, but will offer them understandings that will keep the conversation going and will provide openings for reconciliation, productivity, and peace.

Trust as a Good amid Differences

To speak of positive outcomes that enhance trust is, of course, to assume that trust is a good thing. Such an assumption seems to be so obvious that it hardly needs underscoring. However, many of the philosophers have also taught that one must reckon with and speak of
circumstances and contexts in which there are good reasons to value
distrust and suspicion. The discourse involving the slave and the free,
the oppressor and the victim, the privileged and the disadvantaged cannot be completed by cheerful appeals to dialogue and conversation. Issues of power and justice will remain, and the disparities need to be addressed. The price of naiveté and gullibility in human transactions can
be unimaginably high, whether in matters of government, commerce,
religion, or social institutions. Therefore, when someone who is a
stranger and who brings no credible credentials to a new social environment bids others to some outrageous proposal based on "trust me" appeals, only a fool would extend a hand of assent without first doing
some analyzing, checking, calculating, and recognizing that risk is involved. The scam artists and shysters in the worlds of the Internet and
commerce would have the world to themselves, and everyone else
would lose everything, were all forms of trust in all situations to be, yes,
trusted. Suspicion remains a useful element in the complex of trust and
its opposites and has to be in the toolkit of those who would contribute
to cultures of trust.

Mention of the stranger calls to mind the diversity present in most
societies in our time, diversity that contributes to alienation and conflict. Within ethnic groups, sororities, garden clubs, and the like, people often generate sets of meanings and send signals that make communication easy and can help generate trust. However, when there is
little common history or no record of past dealings, trust is harder to
develop and maintain. The idea of beginning with the concept of distrust or — let us coin a word for momentary use — "nontrust" is the realistic and thus helpful groundwork for building from an understanding of history or the testimony of our own eyes. To be effective, pluralist
societies need leaders who meet head-on the problems these societies
raise for people who have — or think they have — experienced homogeneity and stability within their tradition. Such leaders will ask, Don't
civil societies in which trust is to meet trust have to be based on a wide
and deep consensus among citizens? Atop that question, the student of

history tosses in a complication: while agreement and homogeneity can contribute to a civil society or, in our case, to cultures of trust, they can also portend civil wars and in their cozy world suffer from the absence of creative stimuli from outside sources. The question may be posed more intensely: Don't we have to begin all formulation on the basis of consensus, even despite the risks it implies?

The plot of my book *The One and the Many: America's Search for the Common Good* deals with the theme of such consensus. Numbers of theorists whose writings I consulted on the issues of pluralism reminded readers that polities like that of the United States did not come from leaders or members of a public who trusted each other because they naturally shared a consensus. Many in public religious controversies asked: Weren't almost all the founding fathers Bible-believing Protestants, who thus had few problems of communication and did not suffer threats of societal breakdown? Until I read theorists who were not paralyzed by pluralism, I was tempted to agree with the celebrators of homogeneity. Then I found and was influenced by some thinkers who were realistic about human differences, misunderstanding, conflict, and distrust, but who contributed constructively to the creation and prosperity of civil societies.

Hence, John Courtney Murray, S.J., occasioned some surprise after the middle of the twentieth century when he wrote realistically and at length about how it was instead *dissensus* that gave natural shape to life in a pluralist society. He had a double message: pluralism is here to stay, whether or not the will of God produced it (he believed it went against the will of God, but was in fact the human condition); therefore, in colloquial terms, his implied advice was "get over it." And then he went on to see its potential for enriching a constitutional society such as the American one, which he celebrated. When they were developing structures for life in a constitutional republic and then later elaborating on these, citizens of all kinds and backgrounds, Catholics and Protestants, believers and nonbelievers, proponents of natural law and those who did not find the concept useful, had difficulty finding a *consensus juris,* a basis from which agreement on law could issue. They could not find common articles of faith — ideological or creedal agreement — but they developed and lived with articles of peace, which made it possible for positive consequences to follow. Somehow, despite their *dissensus,* they produced the polity of a republic in which the contenders and contributors just mentioned "conspired" — Murray's term for "breathed together" — sufficiently to produce a non-utopian yet workable constitution and base for the rule of law.[2]

In a sense these founders made a deft maneuver, one that was characteristic of something I discerned by accident when reading an essay by physician-philosopher Lewis Thomas in an essay on erring. In this analogy, "erring" relates to "distrust." Thomas took off from the familiar phrase, part truism and part cliché, that we learn by "trial and error." Note, he said, we do not say that we learn from "trial and triumph." But when we do learn from error, this is not the result of the error or an unreflective response; there had to be conscious intervention. Thus, in the scientific world, someone lets the specimen lie unattended too long, sets the laboratory temperature too high, or feeds wrong calculations into the computer, with the result that error occurs. Now comes the crucial moment, when someone on the scene asks, "Even so, what then?" That question appears at the point at which creativity enters. Knowing in advance but from experience that this is how one often makes discoveries is comparable to what can happen when we say that we "trust through the experience of distrust." So, after incidents or evidences of distrust appear, the key moment is when someone says, "Even so, what then?"[3]

Philosopher Nicholas Rescher, in his writing on pluralism, discusses how publics deal or can deal with the absence or loss of consensus at the base of political society. The historical record in the United States, he showed, did not give evidence that the national founders and the people they served embodied a life of consensus from which an errant and diverse nation had fallen. Starting with consensus, he observed, is not the way social institutions are formed. Especially in their various groups, people demonstrate vastly differing interests — a situation that, by the way, makes "natural trusting" difficult. Societies form when citizen groups acquiesce to others for the good of the whole. In part, it is because they do so that they make possible the development of a civil society. So humans in society never shared an originally satisfactory fabric of trust that was later to be torn apart. They had to invent and cultivate a new one and then keep stitching together such an artifact.

2. John Courtney Murray, S.J., *We Hold These Truths: Catholic Reflections on the American Proposition* (New York: Sheed and Ward, 1960), pp. 56ff.

3. For a development of this theme, see my "'But Even So, Look at That': An Ironic Perspective on Utopias," in *Visions of Utopia,* ed. Edward Rothstein, Herbert Muschamp, Martin E. Marty (New York: Oxford University Press, 2003), pp. 49-88.

By the time of the War of Independence, citizens in disparate and often contending colonies learned that they had to get together against the British foe. Doing so demanded that they acquiesce in some of the demands that they once could have made back in the luxury of their mutual isolation. Now they had to begin to find ways to trust each other as they began to have a common national life. The phrase in the Declaration of Independence proclaiming that "we hold these truths to be self-evident" represents a written parallel to what we might call an "even so, what then?" moment in the formation and passage of the Constitution. The authors demonstrated that they knew that societies that take for granted the potential for distrust, or deal with the actual presence of significant distrust, can still be productive of human good. Historical illustrations like that one have inspired others. Various peoples have found ways to deal with their natural mistrust as they have developed structures and profited from events that emphasized the values and realities of cultures of trust.

Prehuman, Prehumanistic Evidences

We may well ask: On what bases, other than those derived from the scriptures, can we be dismissive of the views of human nature that depend on a belief in progress toward perfectibility as the basis on which trust can develop? Among the main choices in our culture are some anthropological-evolutionary inquiries to go with the religious and philosophical. Anthropological and ethological approaches, so favored today, find scientists making assessments of the "native" character of the trusting or mistrusting brain. Why not consider humans to be naturally and essentially trustworthy? Since I am building my case on ambiguities and contradictions in life, I have to pay some attention to the current status of arguments concerning the question of selfish violence versus generosity, or of posing savagery over against kindness or, in our context, mistrust over against trust.

For the generations since World War II, and in a time when scholars of all kinds have been trying to account for the roots of human aggression, lethal action, violent behavior, and the impulses that lead to them, the main claim has been that savagery was the dominant ancestral expression. In vogue in our time — and certainly not to be dismissed — are emphases on the selfish gene. In this vein, evolution-oriented philosophers such as Richard Dawkins have suggested that even apparent altruism is just that — apparent. By some instinct, the prairie dog presents himself as a noisemaker who attracts predators at the cost of his life. He does so, say students of the selfish gene, so that his collegial puppies can scramble for cover. But the self-sacrificer is dismissed as little more than a cog in the evolutionary machine. In the dog-eat-prairie-dog world, no being can trust any other, leading to the conclusion: Have we humans changed all that much in our evolved stage and status?

Such findings and testimony have not been universally supportive of the "don't trust" side, and, to keep nurturing ambiguity, I adduce challenges to the picture of integral mistrust in the animal world. Frans de Waal, a professor of primate behavior at Emory University, has notably claimed that the dominant school has not dealt satisfactorily with "the mystery of aggression." For years he and his colleagues have observed, gathered, and presented data of a kind different from what has ruled in common opinion. Among evidences that impressed members of his school were observations of Binti Jua, a female gorilla who made headlines by rescuing a child at a zoo in Chicago. Students of primate behavior who were made aware of instances like this had to look again and then revise some theories — or at least entertain the idea of revising them.[4]

The bonobo, one of four ape species, especially shows traces of trustworthy and generous behavior. It had been assumed by many experts that Chimp Number One in each company achieved his status by being powerful, vicious, and selfish. De Waal's team observed bonobos that are evidently of a different kind. Some of them, he noted, create mutually beneficial ties to other bonobos with whom they are affiliated and in contact. They use gestures, he argues, that should be studied more carefully by observers of human behavior than they usually are. The key word in de Waal's report on bonobos is "affiliation," which, as readers can picture, is a major constituent in associational or cultural proposals for laying down new bases for trust.

One specialty in the de Waal camp is the observation of "social

---

4. Frans de Waal, *The Forgotten Ape* (Berkeley: University of California Press, 2008). For the references to ethological research that I cite in the next several pages, see also David Berreby, "Are Apes Naughty by Nature?" *New York Times,* Jan. 26, 2007, and Natalie Angier, "In Most Species, Faithfulness Is a Fantasy," *New York Times,* March 18, 2008.

grooming." One could, of course, write off such companionate or —
dare we say? — collegial activities and see them as merely pragmatic
and selfishly prudential. Mutual groomers seem better positioned for
sexual activities, and along the way they want to be able to count on
their companions who have shared the grooming experience. Mention
of the de Waal observations on this subject is not sufficient to settle the
argument; but as the research grows apace, criticism from standard-
brand ethological behaviorists is given more notice.

For those who wonder why this side trip (or back trip!) to primates
and their behavior comes up in a chapter on humanistic resources, my
answer is that it alerts readers to the ambiguities in these schools of observation. This is not the place for an amateur to feign expertise on
technical subjects such as on how "Beta-endorphin concentrations in
cerebrospinal fluid in monkeys are influenced by grooming relationships." For me, the study typically calls for a cautionary note, one that in
effect warns against being wholly committed to either deterministic visions of human mistrust or utopian visions of trust, even before humans are on the scene.

Instead, we can more cautiously observe the way embodiments of
"the selfish gene" can help encourage understanding among those who
would build structures of trust. These examples occur between the
mother, who must be "trusted" to return to the nest with food for her offspring, and the offspring, who somehow "trust" their mother to bring
food. There may be times when some forms of trust appear in the animal
world beyond parent-and-child relationships, but in the world of predators and their victims, the smaller and weaker beings who trust the
larger and stronger are often soon killed and eaten. Mark Twain, having
read the prophecy of a paradisiacal kingdom in which the lion would lie
down with the lamb, remarked that such an arrangement would work if
one had a vast supply of lambs. Most of the energy in animal family relations goes into building up defenses, creating distances, or working out
strategies that assume that no one not of their kind — and often even *of*
their kind — is to be trusted. One can appeal to little in that animal-
ancestral world as a basis for proving that trust was natural and prevalent in the prehuman, or other-than-human, animal world.

Of more interest than the primate ancestry of violence is that of sexual relations, an area that has elicited almost playful elaborations.
Citing one or another of the ethologists might add weight to our observation that distrust, not trust, prevails in the world of what is consid-

ered "natural" in sexual matters, so important in human discourse about trust. The press has learned to be quick to connect troubling headline news with scientific research on sexual trust and mistrust in the primate world. The most celebrated recent interest was the exposure of hypocrisy and sexual transgression on the part of Governor Eliot Spitzer of New York, who, though married and a public opponent of prostitution, was charged with having patronized prostitutes for years. Science writer Natalie Angier quickly picked up the subject in the *New York Times* in a piece headlined "In Most Species, Faithfulness Is a Fantasy." She asked whether nonhuman animals can trust their kind. "Sexual promiscuity is rampant throughout nature, and true faithfulness a fond fantasy," she says. Angier acknowledges that some animals form "pair bonds" and keep confirming them. Yet biologists who apply DNA paternity testing find that "social monogamy is very rarely accompanied by sexual, or genetic, monogamy."

Finally, and grippingly, husband and wife co-authors David P. Barash and Judith Eve Lipton, in their book *The Myth of Monogamy,* claim to have found only one species in which monogamy is universal: the *Diplozoon paradoxum,* a flatworm that lives in the gills of freshwater fish. Once bonded, they do not need trust because they have no risk — and cannot have any. Barash and Lipton write: "Males and females meet each other as adolescent, and their bodies literally fuse together, whereupon they remain faithful until death."[5] Angier reports that, in certain species of baboons, males or females who "cheat" suffer a physical response: "[M]ost female baboons have lost half an ear here, a swatch of pelt there, to the jealous fury of their much larger and toothier males." In many species there is "zealous partner policing," which leads the reporters to close with an application to the human mistrust scene: "Be warned, you big lounge lizard: it could happen to you."

Back to the Human Scene and Humanistic Studies

There may be just a large enough number of exceptions to the observations of savage and faithless instances among species to keep us from universalizing the experience. There is also enough sustained and con-

---

5. David P. Barash and Judith Eve Lipton, *The Myth of Monogamy: Fidelity and Infidelity in Animals and People* (New York: W. H. Freeman, 2008).

firmed research that limits the potential of trading on them to come up with sunny views of primate and other nonhuman ancestry. Instead, we will move expeditiously from primatology back to the study of the human species, the proper subject for historians. With Jacob Burckhardt, I will not rely on a philosophy of history so much as observations of the human, starting out "from the one point accessible to us, the one eternal center of all things — man, suffering, striving, doing, as he is and was and ever shall be."[6] And since the human is a thinking animal, it is proper to concentrate on those who think about thinking animals.

Among philosophers, trust has not received the explicit attention one might have expected concerning such a basic topic. However, as anticipated above, in classical philosophy Plato, whom we cited as an originator, did take it up. In *The Republic* he sets an agenda for later and lesser thinkers. Few serious students of trust proceed without attention to this classic, a virtual book of Genesis on the subject. The view of human nature offered in *The Republic* by Glaucon, Plato's brother (in dialogue with Socrates), is so pessimistic that it almost makes Christian talk about the Fall and original sin sound cheering. In the dialogue we meet Glaucon as someone who knows about human nature and who brings enough sense of suspicion to be useful to realists throughout history. He knows that, after the passage of a law, authorities will punish violators. At the same time, with such law and threat in force, an implicit understanding of trust will appear, which says, "We legislators have passed the law, and we trust you citizens to keep it." Depending on the law and the character of the state, many — even most — citizens do keep trust. Why? The answer is easy for Glaucon to grasp: the law stipulates penalties, and one who is caught breaking the law will be punished. In sum it is simple: fear of that potential punishment produces what looks like a trust-keeping response.

Glaucon illustrates his point with one of the more familiar parables in philosophy. In this story, a shepherd named Gyges finds a ring that grants him a particular magical power. If, while wearing it, he chooses to twist it, he becomes invisible. Given this instrument, Gyges sets out on a course of criminal and devastating action. Soon he kills the king, after which he seizes the throne and the queen. Glaucon, spinning out his philosophy of life and his observation of human conduct on this ba-

---

6. Jacob Burckhardt, *Force and Freedom: An Interpretation of History*, ed. James Hastings Nichols (New York: Meridian Books, 1955), p. 71.

sis, argues that all the rest of us would do precisely what Gyges does if we had access to the same magical equipment and fell into an identical circumstance, no matter how disciplined and moral we are in our visible, and thus observed, lives. Fear of getting caught and being punished is the only motor for trust-bearing action. There is in our make-up, according to Glaucon, no natural impulse for or interest at all in being moral and trustworthy. Gyges's story's bearing on the concept of trust is so heavy that it deserves retelling in Plato's words:

> No man would keep his hands off what was not his own when he could safely take what he liked out of the market, or go into houses and lie with any one at his pleasure, or kill or release from prison whom he would, and in all respects be like a God among men. Then the actions of the just would be as the actions of the unjust; they would both come at last to the same point. And this we may truly affirm to be a great proof that a man is just, not willingly or because he thinks that justice is any good to him individually, but of necessity, for whenever any one thinks that he can safely be unjust, there he is unjust. For all men believe in their hearts that injustice is far more profitable to the individual than justice, and he who argues as I have been supposing, will say that they are right.[7]

Totalitarians, leaders of police states, hard-liners in the surveillance business, and not a few analysts of human behavior simply agree with Glaucon. In his view, what looks like trust is merely an action based on a circumstance in which there is no risk. However, were the person in question visible, there would be risk, since he might be caught. Who would risk punishment, given such circumstances? Yet, whoever pictures himself as invisible and undetectable need never trust because, in such circumstances, he would have the assurance that he could do anything — such as break trust. While doing so, he could escape detection and thus punishment. Basing calculations on Glaucon's view in Plato, a customer could count on the merchant not to overcharge or deliver an inferior product because some governmental agency would catch him price-fixing, or a bureau of standards would penalize him for low quality.

---

7. *The Dialogues of Plato,* ed. B. Jowett (New York: Random House, 1937), vol. 1, 623-24. This Glaucon episode is in *The Republic,* 2: 359-60.

Whenever I genuinely do trust, I am "sticking my neck out" and taking a risk. Fear of getting caught for breaking a trust is my guarantee that what I do will make me look trustworthy. In its depth, a jungle mentality colors Glaucon's view, since it presumes that little "Trusting Me" will have exposed myself to harm, and "the other," the one with whom I am dealing, will bring about harm. So I come to the conclusion that I must arm myself and take aggressive defensive action, which will be met by defensive aggressive counteraction, and this will start a contest of suspicions, wills, resources, and energies. Those afflicted with Glauconism engage in preemptive strikes against potential predators. We can see here how, in Plato's view, a rationale for the invention of the state as an instrument of defense was forthcoming. Aside from what the state can do to provide a surrogate for the trust that is impossible to gain and sustain, it is capable of making heroes out of villains and can provide a scenario in which, among the professionals, arms manufacturers can profit the most.

Plato's Glaucon classically summarizes a view of trust that is picked up frequently in later philosophy. It suggests that, since life is short and potential philosophical ideas are almost limitless, philosophers have to be selective, to pick subjects worthy of their sustained attention. Why, we may ask, should they concern themselves with trust? The primatologist has her reasons, as we have seen, as does the banker or the person pledging vows of marriage. But the philosopher? To provide elements of an answer, count on pragmatic philosophers to ask, "Of what use is contemplation on trust?" Further, they ask how such a philosophical theme might cash out in "real life."

A moment's reflection can lead to fresh understandings as to why this classic but still undertreated subject belongs in philosophy. Trust broken, mistrust, and distrust have their obvious practical effects in many professions. Thus, military leaders have coercive means of attracting compliance when they offer trust: failure to take orders from superiors can lead to severe punishment for trust-breaking subordinates. The same leaders have to count on the degree of confidence they can have in their allies when they proffer trust and when they bid for cooperation and coalition.

Similarly, business agents, for all their reliance on legally monitored contracts, still put great energy into winning trust and risking it on someone else. Beyond that, they rely on relatively trustworthy experiences of a firm with which they choose to associate. They count on friendship bonds cultivated among each other as mutual alumni/ae of the same alma mater. Or they make risk assessments that can occur among church or club members, evidenced by handshakes among partners and friends, to make their world of commerce function. As they express and receive signs of trust, they testify that they grow through their risk and dependency on it. A culture of trust, though still weak and vulnerable, begins to develop.

Attach to it the issue of what the frequent and profound evidences of trusting in trust can do for the people who transact with it. They profess to grow in confidence and courage every time they venture to extend more. When two people develop a relationship of trust and then invent some means to prevent themselves from deserting it when it makes high demands, they are contributing to cultures of trust as they rob the subversive, underground, suspicious, and self-glorying agents of "go it alone" philosophies of distrust. The more the circle of trusters and the trustworthy can grow, the more it will contribute to what philosophers speak of as "the common good." Of course, as philosophers consider trust a good, they are helping to build cultures of trust.

Help from Hobbes and His Contemporaries

If Plato framed our first set of reflections inspired by philosophy, a number of early modern thinkers identified with the Enlightenment show that they also assume that distrust and being untrustworthy are more natural expressions than are their opposites. One is not likely to proceed far in discussions of the philosophy of trust on the grounds of human nature without ending in the depths with Hobbes. On rational grounds, he sets the reader up to picture the transactions within marriage and the family, in commerce and education — and religion! — as offering very little. To begin to meet the problems, Hobbes pictures the creative role of the state, of laws, and of truces in his work *Leviathan.* Without such provisions, the stateless human would live out his life in a state of nature among other people who also live out their lives in a state of nature. Picturing life without imposed restraints on conduct, it would be "every man against every man," with the consequence that the lives of all would be "solitary, poor, nasty, brutish, and short" and, be it noted, unmarked by trust or the conditions for trusting.

Hobbes argues that, if life has been apparently improved in a day marked by truce and trust, the state at its best is an instrument capable of extending trust into the future. Thus the practice and habit of trusting can be prolonged and partly realized. Viewed negatively, this means that humans will refrain from acting on the basis of their brutish nature. Such a response, in turn, means that they will be kept from killing each other and will be "trusted" to let others live. Of course, if trust on this basis breaks down, people will return to efforts to kill each other and take from others what they have wanted all along. Such a basis for trust is not very glamorous or flattering to human nature. Put another way, it is very "Hobbesian"; but, Hobbes would say, "Consider the alternatives," given what we know about humans.

At each stage the cautious but hopeful reader is tempted to say: "That's it! What we have just described as the beginning of his address to the problem is a sufficient base for assuring trust." Yet Hobbes does not rest; he pushes back even further. His premise, or the one he evokes in readers' minds, is that humans are so selfish, frail, and guided by something other than reason, that they may forget the implicit rules of the game in order to advance self-interest. People do not act or calculate actions rationally, he argues, and they often exceed the bounds of their implicit truces and trusts. Seeking to take advantage of the other, each will act aggressively.

Here is the basis for wars among humans: even in the best thought-out circumstance, there will be violators of truces or boundaries. And here is where profound cynicism verging on hopelessness takes over: since the "other" might at any time jump the gun and take advantage of me, it is in my self-interest to jump the gun to take advantage of the enemy. Those are the roots of the preemptive strikes that become part of warfare — or of all features of war in general. So long as one is ahead of the game and can take advantage of that head start or amassing of power, he might be expected to act, and to act aggressively. The endgame here offers little hope for extended truce, less hope for trust, and little hope in general.

At this point the other philosopher whose name occurs in all such accounts of modern life makes an appearance: David Hume. His *A Treatise of Human Nature* deals with human interests in the impulse to find company, even the possibility of receiving love. Yet whoever invests too much hope in ready improvements in human encounters and engagements will be disappointed by Hume, who throws more hurdles on the

track of the optimists. Among those who find company and love are —
or should be — members of families. Yet family quarrels can be of the
worst kind. Anthropologist Bronislaw Malinowski wisely notes that aggression, like charity, begins at home.[8] Members of families know secrets about each other, make pledges and break them, and are nearest
at hand when hostile or vengeful impulses rule. Those who agree with
Hume will note that sympathy, company, and love of one's own often
breeds hostility to the "other."

Grimly realistic but unwilling to give up in a quest for trust, Hume
and any number of colleagues pressed on to present fresh rationales for
pursuing it. With intellectual and spiritual darkness visible around
them, they celebrated what came to be called the *Aufklärung,* or Enlightenment. Hume was a leader in touting intellectual improvement,
which, for him, meant the use of reason in ways that move situations
beyond the scope of mere rational calculation. He and his colleagues
posited the idea that in the society of the future, natural law, natural
reason, and natural religion might find a place, since among reason-
able and reasoning people they would help minimize risk. What the
philosophers of this school came up with, however, is not likely to be
called trust or a solution to the trust problem. Hobbes proposed self-
policing policies, most prominently the "social contract," a contributor
to the development of a restrictive kind of culture of trust.

During the same period, a drastically different approach emerged
that can be applied to the pursuit of trust: Immanuel Kant's "categorical imperative," which concentrated not on the social order but on the
ethic of the person. Kant's starting point, in many ways the opposite of
Hobbes's and Hume's, posited the rational and autonomous individual, a figure of dignity and potential responsibility. People, instead of
operating defensively to protect themselves from self-centered and
predatory folks, he argued, should act on the basis of a principle that
could be universalized. This means that it had to be designed to work
for people in all cultures. The imperative called for a person to act in
such a way that the action could be applicable to and usable by all. The
corollary to this imperative demanded that persons should not use
other persons, should not treat them as being of no intrinsic value, but
only as being useful to their own ends, not as means.

8. Bronislaw Malinowski, "An Anthropological Analysis of War," in *Magic, Science,
and Religion* (Glencoe, IL: Free Press, 1948), p. 285.

Here was a fresh ground for promoting trust. Kant argued that, if you offered to be trustworthy and kept the promises you had made, you *must* be trustworthy. If you offered trust and did not plan to follow through, you were engaging in an act that could not morally be followed by anyone else, and you would have failed to keep to the categorical imperative. Picture a world in which false bids and promises for trust are widespread, and you will be depicting chaos, the breakdown of all social order. Turning this over, the more that people make promises and keep them, the more they will develop networks and what I am calling "cultures of trust," and even whole societies would grow in stability and value.

In the scope of Kant's prescription, transactions of trust enlarge responsibilities, enhance expressions of trust, and thus benefit all. Beginning from his imperative at least gives a base for some compromise, whereas starting with promises that use people as means, not toward good ends, is simply destructive. In Kant's thinking, a compromising idealist and moral person provides a better situation than would a person who has no values in the first place.

The props that many thinkers have brought in to support trust have remained — and still remain — variations of Hobbes's social-contract theory. Since they and he could not base trust on the natural goodness of humans, they moved to promote human equality and freedom. The move was radical: people can trust each other, he argued, because they contract to do so. And this is the case because in a way they choose the authority that, in those days and Hobbes's thought, usually meant the monarch. To be credible, the participants in organizing this sovereign power, which is to help assure trust-keeping, must be chosen freely by free people. No alternatives to that will work.

No one gets to relax at this point in a philosophical argument because, as critics of Hobbes and others point out, freely chosen contracts can be freely broken on the grounds of safeguarding human autonomy. Ungrounded in natural law or human nature, such contracts seem unmoored, as if chosen by whim and dismissible on even slight and perhaps idiosyncratic grounds. Because agreements last beyond the moment they were made and are formally chosen by only some of the people, everyone within a polity can protest, "I did not participate in organizing and supporting this authority. Leave me out!"

A Contemporary Counsel and Trust in Information

These references might suggest that philosophical discussions of trust began in ancient Greece and ended in Western Europe in the eighteenth century. While trust talk has often been neglected by philosophers, it has come back and is likely to receive ever-increasing attention. The most-discussed example of recent revisionist talk is a book by Onora O'Neill that includes her Gifford Lectures and her Reith Lectures for the BBC in 2002. A professor in the United States until 1977, O'Neill did her mature work at Essex and Cambridge universities. In the Reith Lectures, O'Neill confesses that she had long neglected trust, but she found that personal experiences and observations prompted her to engage it formally. She heard the common claim that what was called "the crisis of trust" was usually and prematurely reduced to the charge that the occasion for the crisis was the untrustworthiness of others. The new situation in which she wrote was the development of new and efficient instruments of surveillance. Right from the beginning of her investigation she proposed that the efforts to improve trust by improving surveillance and accounting in "our new culture of accountability" were "taking us in the wrong direction," and that British society, by "imposing ever more stringent forms of control," was "busy prescribing copious draughts of the wrong medicine."

In a much-noted climactic passage in her diagnosis, Baroness O'Neill concludes:

> Our revolution in accountability has not reduced attitudes of mistrust, but rather reinforced a culture of suspicion. Instead of working towards intelligent accountability based on good governance, independent inspection and careful reporting, we are galloping towards central planning by performance indicators, reinforced by obsessions with blame and compensation. This is pretty miserable both for those who feel suspicious and for those who are suspected of untrustworthy action — sometimes with little evidence.[9]

This apt diagnosis led O'Neill to take a fresh approach in the Reith Lectures, one that she calls a "much more practical view of trust." While

9. Onora O'Neill made these comments on BBC Radio in 2002, referring to her broadcasts and her *Autonomy and Trust in Bioethics* (Cambridge: Cambridge University Press, 2002).

stepping back from a "controls" approach, she shows that she is not interested in anything that is casual and that does not take mistrust seriously. She does not advocate "blind trust" or ignorant, thoughtless, and careless trust-giving. One promotes a culture of trust, she argues, by first doing everything possible to give the public the most honest and best information on the basis of which they make decisions. She trots on stage Samuel Johnson: "It is better to be sometimes cheated than never to have trusted," a theme that is in place after O'Neill or anyone else in this line reminds us that there are, finally, no guarantees. Recalling that her focus is on professions more than on day-to-day transactions in "ordinary" life, we might extend them to the larger scene through the creation of subcultures of trust.

Cultures of trust come in many sizes, forms, levels, and thicknesses. On the assumption that we can make the most promising contribution by specializing on aspects of only two or three of the most influential, we will follow up on O'Neill's address to some professions. This focus will be useful when we discuss how professionals in science, religion, and politics communicate or fail to do so, grow suspicious or trustful — and what their approaches will mean for their constituents and the public. Through the subcultures in which they work, builders of trust can reach larger publics. Thus, if there is a breakdown of trust that affects schools, media, religious institutions, government, and the like, we must turn to the professions if they are to help provide "the most honest and best information on the basis of which [members of the public] make decisions."

Whoever reads the history of conflict and confusion where science, religion, and public life intersect will find that specialists, experts, and concentrators on one or another of these spheres tend to develop modes of inquiry, theories, experiments, and practices that become remote from the experience in others. To call it a problem of communication is to point to a necessary but not sufficient issue. Improved communication and understanding will not mean an end to conflict or a soft blend across lines of disciplines. It can mean keeping the conversation going so that there are more openings for showing empathy, promoting cooperation, and taking up issues common to all in the larger public.

Reinforcing Trust Habitually

Reflection on the humanistic traditions can point to one important area that I have not yet discussed, but that thinkers from Aristotle to John Dewey have emphasized: *habit in conduct.* When one travels in a distant land, where the traveler knows no one and no one knows the traveler, the risks that come with professions offering trust are higher than they were within a known culture of trust. The traveler may be gone from the scene in a day or three, so there are no prudential reasons for the one offering trust to befriend the visitor in order to get something out of her in the future. Travelers regularly speak of merchants or police who take advantage of them. Others report gestures and acts that are not born of prudence or affection but because there is something in the impulse of the generous extenders of trust that cannot be denied and that, one discerns, can be counted on or has been evident. Enlarging the number and increasing the visibility of people who can be trusted in such circumstances is a further means to enhance trust-relations in a precarious world.

Even people who are suspicious and have reason to be so are likely to make hundreds of decisions per day based on trust-relations. Anyone who learns from Aristotle cheers whenever trust-keeping becomes habitual.[10] But to be told about the value of trust does less for the subject than practicing it does. Alfred North Whitehead at one point in his argument suggests that ordinary lives are marked by decisions and actions based on, first, routine and then, second, on understanding.[11] His reference is to whole societies, but we can bring the issue closer to home by noting personal life. Tying one's shoes in the morning ordinarily belongs to routine, and the one who ties expeditiously in ten seconds can be off to work and play, not having wasted intellectual energy on the action. However, if the shoestring breaks and needs replacement, or a sore hand handicaps the potential shoe-tier, he must shift strategy and practice to relocate the subject where the category "understanding" applies. Of course, the sooner he can turn the matter back to routine, the better off the shod person will be,

---

10. *The Ethics of Aristotle: The Nicomachean Ethics,* ed. and trans. J. A. K. Thomason (New York: Penguin, 1976), pp. 336-37.

11. Alfred North Whitehead, *Adventures of Ideas* (New York: Mentor Books, 1953), pp. 96-98.

as he can then devote "understanding" to intellectual matters that have consequences.

Extending or inviting trust comes down to a combination of a state of mind and rational calculation. "Things do not add up," one says, if calculation based only on intuition, or certainly only on bad records of performance, suggests that when trust is needed, something about the "other" makes a person uneasy. This uneasiness may be rooted in reality: if there has been a shared past, positive experiences are vital. Uneasiness can turn to suspicion and, in extreme cases, to paranoia. In such instances, distrust grows, paradoxically, the more a party makes attempts to dispel it, explain it away, or assure someone else that there is no reason to be distrustful. The person with paranoia asks, "How do I know about and have assurance when the next instance of interaction will present itself?" The necessarily unknown character of the future events means to the afflicted — or even to any moderately suspicious person — that she must keep her guard up. The only help she can envision in such circumstances is the participation of both in a culture of trust, where the habits of trusting are consistent and thus liberating.

In every kind of case, as the two parties assess each other, the one who is asked to trust — or who would like to trust — looks at the other with an effort to try to calculate: Why is this person ready for trust, given all the risks? Or, why is he ready to risk on me? What motives and attitudes should I project and is he counting on? Let me illustrate. Two friends have gone fishing for a week in a remote lake area. On the second day, one asks the other, "What is your wife doing tonight?"

"I haven't the faintest idea."

"Oh, come on," replies the questioner. "That can't be true. I've never heard of anything like that: a husband, far from home and not easily accessible, and he claims not to know what his wife is doing?"

The questioned one reaffirms that he has no idea what his wife is doing.

"If you don't know what she is doing," asks the questioner, "how can you trust her? There are so many things a woman on her own can do to get into trouble or give you trouble. You should be sure you know. Take me: I want to trust my wife, so I keep track of her." When his friend asks how he can do that, he says: "Well, last night after we got to the lake, and you were putting gear in the boat, I called my wife on the cell phone. I was calling just to make sure she wasn't up to something. She was indeed at home. What's more, tonight is her night for bridge, so that's taken care of: she and I would surely hear about it if she didn't take her place in that foursome. To give you a bit of security, let me tell you what *your* wife is doing tomorrow. She's going to a concert with my wife. Look, I have all six evenings covered. I told you, I want to be sure of her. I want to trust her."

The listening friend in the boat simply ends the conversation by saying that he does not have to call or keep track because the two members of the couple have a record, a bond based on a pledge, a way of signaling their trust in each other, that gives him assurance. This couple has created a two-person culture of trust. The philosophers would conclude that this wife is a good risk, and both partners are expert trustees. Are either of them 100 percent sure of the other? One never can be, since human beings are the subject here. Yet one can be sure that there is experience and security enough to inspire confidence: here is a good bet.

I expect that everyone who has heard or read this story can understand and will even anticipate someone interrupting this way: "Enough! Even we amateur psychologists know about all this, and we don't need to have reports on the conversation in the boat repeated endlessly." So it is with trust. Whoever reflects — meaning, whoever puts understanding to work too much of the time — will not be free or focused to invest in acts that do demand reflection. Anyone who is not paranoid, not in enemy territory, nor in situations where "Do Not Trust Anyone!" signs have to be posted, would do well to be reflective. And the reflective one would be astonished to fill a notebook with all the instances in which a productive person has to trust and can trust. For example, a driver has to trust that the driver of an oncoming car does not drift across the center-line stripes and crash head-on into his car. The driver cannot be absolutely certain that such a lethal intrusion will not happen because there are many accidents attributable to lane-crossings each year. Yet any driver may face thousands of cars in any particular day, and if his concern is staying far from the center line, he may endanger other autos moving in his direction and in his own lanes. There can be more danger from hypercautious drivers in one's own traffic lanes than from that one in millions of oncoming cars.

It would be difficult to build cultures of trust if all the members of those cultures had to scurry back to the Bible or Plato for direction in each assessment of the human condition where matters of trust come up. Similarly, to have to start from scratch on rationalist grounds and calculate what the Kantian categorical imperative means — or to calculate why we should set up and sign social contracts in the mode of Hobbes and Hume — would produce results that would be unnecessarily unstable and evanescent. If there is to be trust, one has to be seen as habitually trustworthy, and the one to whom that trust is extended must see the other as such. Similarly, if one is to trust a teacher or an educational system, a financial institution or a trader, a culture of trust will rely on institutions with long records of habitual trust-keeping.

We can illustrate this by observing companies or clubs in which trust develops and is exemplified. When one can say of those in a company or a club, at a time when they are being tempted, "That just isn't done around here," it projects an image that reflects a reality and contributes to a richer situation. What the listener hears is: "That isn't done around here; so you can trust us." Evidence of trust-keeping is open for examination. That the act of relying on a tradition of trustworthy practices heightens risk is obvious. Failure to live up to the expectation implicitly being advertised would lead to a devastating setback for those trust-breakers who act against a pattern of good habits. Offering and keeping trust are hence to be seen as both morally and practically efficient activities.

Social philosophers who would make the case for building trust typically do so by pointing to what happens when trust breaks down. Most of those philosophers spend less time dealing with trust in the abstract than they do pointing out the social costs of untrustworthiness and broken trust. In popular settings — for example, in spectator sports — they point to those fans who identify with certain iconic teams and players. These publics are shaken when they find that there has been point-shaving, gambling, steroid use, the stealing of team signals, and other scandalous behavior. While all illegal behavior, when exposed, will offend the sensibilities of the law-abiding members of the public, they will be most roused when a player or a team they have supported betrays their confidence.

On a more technical level, but one that can be a life-and-death matter for ordinary citizens, we observe what occurs when someone betrays trust in the scientific and medical fields. Most of what goes on in scientific research is beyond the comprehension or testing ability of the very lay public that will depend on the outcomes of research by the professionals, for example, the life-giving or death-dealing potentials of some pharmaceuticals. Someone in a laboratory who juggles statistics or makes false claims is eventually found out by others who try to replicate her experiments and find her claims faulty. The Glaucon principle operates here: some apparent integrity is enforced in a scientist who fears she will be found out by those who check her data. This is something one cannot readily do in religion, if the reference point is the transcendent deity. Still, the priests and theologians who engage in misconduct can be caught as readily as can those in other professions.

Harder to catch in the act than laboratory scientists are inventors of price-fixing schemes of large drug companies. When a trusted firm is caught in illegal or borderline immoral actions, a crisis of confidence occurs: executives are fired, shares in the company decline in value, and, worst of all, sick people are denied reliable products and counsel. Once again, the philosopher who deals with the qualities of trust and how to advance them will find immediate concrete illustrations interrupting an abstract case. This means that the cause of philosophy in society is advanced because the ethical lapses are compensated for by better watchdog activities, which can lead to less need for watchdogging. The goals of much pragmatic philosophical thought on trust are to improve the production of social life, in whose spheres transactions occur and individuals develop trustworthiness. Once again, the product is a culture of trust, or an advance toward achieving one.

Risk and Rationality

The mention of risk brings us to focus on another factor, something that is central in cultures of trust. Philosophical discussions of trust can never escape the issue of contingency, which is most regularly and notably connected with risk. The reason for this is obvious, but often forgotten: in the absence of risk, no trust would be necessary. Without risk, the interaction of two parties would represent "having," while trust itself means "hoping to have" or "expecting to have." Risk increases or decreases dependence on the record of the individuals or structures involved and the richness of the climate in the culture of trust in question. The more trust comes to characterize individual and social life, the less morally and financially expensive it is, since the larger society does not have to put so much energy and resources into policing against norm-breaking. Nor does such a culture of trust lead its members to suffer the economic or other costs that result from low production in situations of high security. This is why larger societies often show concern about the quantity and quality, the pulse and heat, of trust.

"Risk" is one of the most prominent terms to show up in philosophical discourse on trust. One hardly needs a philosopher to point out the logic of definition, but philosophers make it clear, once again, to reinforce the point: where there is assurance, or where there are warrants and guarantees, one need not trust. Admittedly, it is hard to picture the achievement of total assurance and thus the removal of all occasions for trust, but for philosophical reasons we must accept such a possible realization. The occasions where risk is a factor vary depending on what kinds of institutions are involved. Governments, universities, and brokerages involve different kinds of risks than do those involving a spouse, an advisor, a comrade-in-arms, or a parent, because those interpersonal versions allow face-to-face appraisals. Still, even institutions that are hard to appraise must beckon for trust; therefore, even in them, the issue finally comes down to the development of responsible persons and their creative philosophies and reliable actions. A CEO or university president who breaks trust threatens the integrity and sometimes even the survival of the institution of which he or she is steward and custodian.

To the philosopher, the problem is how to see expressions of trust — which *are* in some senses placing a bet — as something other than gambling. Trust always has to do with the future, and every analytic philosopher of history knows that we can know nothing in detail and with assurance about the future. Certainly, in commonsense ways, some aspects of the future are "known" to us. The worker "knows" that he will be at an office or factory at, say, nine o'clock on Monday morning. He knows that he and his coworkers will interact in certain preordained ways, perhaps sometimes hierarchically and sometimes democratically. He is confident that there will be a paycheck on a certain day, that he and his family will spend some weekend time at the beach, that he will pay income taxes on or before April 15. He can "count on" all of that, can "trust" that these rhythms will recur. Indeed, some measure of trust is revealed in all this: an employer trusts that the worker will come to work and perform well. His family in the broad sense trusts that he will provide for them and take leisure with them. Yet, on the larger scene, safe as matters seem to be, there is anything but total assurance that, in an economy in crisis, the U.S. government, the Federal Reserve, the SEC, or any number of other agencies will be able to deliver.

Thus, in recent America, citizens of New Orleans showed trust or were forced to trust. They had nothing to work with but trust. They had trusted when they counted on government-built levees not breaking. They were led to trust that the federal government would be of extensive help with recovery after the hurricane did hit, and that New Orleanians could soon resume ordinary life. One could write the whole history of Hurricane Katrina as a social event: once the actual storm died down, citizens found that very little should have been trusted, even in this society where one trusts that constant and generous aid would be coming from public and private sources. What the United States government had failed to do was its part in generating a culture of trust within which citizen transactions could occur with some confidence that victims would be treated honorably. Leaving aside the local and state government failures and staying with our brief case study: it is not news to report that the failure by the federal government to keep implicit and then explicit pledges of trust helped create a devastating crisis of trust.

So, is trust just a game of chance with its own set of rules? What good, one might ask, is trust if institutions on which you depend are there when you do not need them but not there when you do? Absolutists and perfectionists, with unrealistic expectations and lack of self-knowledge, make poor candidates to be trusters. Should some of them take risks and later find themselves abandoned to mistreatment and broken promises, they will be even worse candidates the next time a challenge comes, since experience has matched ideology in their minds. In our envisioning and observing of cultures of trust, we may observe or reason that the more frequently and firmly one has experienced commitments of trust lived up to, the more the capacity to trust grows and the more frequently and profound is the betrayal a person has experienced, the less of a foundation remains on which to build a platform for increasing trust.

Psychological Factors

A whole range of psychological and existential factors can be at play in trust-relations. The paranoid personality, by clinical definition, cannot be a truster. The cynic whose cynicism has been born of the perceived failure of others to affirm him demonstrates again how the ability to trust and the cultivation of a culture of trust are demanding ventures. Those who are to be mentored in this field have to be given some encouragement, but they also have to experience at least *some* occasions when trust is rewarded. Broken trust in the aftermath of firm commitments is analogous to physical abuse. The one who is often beaten flinches even when she hears the footstep of a potential abuser, or when a shadow falls on her path. In all these cases, one observes the passage from trust as a philosophical subject to mistrust as a psychological experience.

It is not only psychologists who ask why someone trusts, is trustworthy, or wants to be considered someone who can be trusted. Here the possibilities are limitless, but many are worth pursuing. We can picture a certain "cosmic" or "ontological" truster, someone who has a bent for moral living and a devotion to ethics. That is, he humbly believes, however small his role, that his part in the universe is integral to the process of holding it together. In practice, of course, he cuts down that imagined universe to local and personal size. However, in this case there has to be a developed belief that being trustworthy makes possible a personal contribution to the integrity of things. Even if no one else attracts trust, he must do so for intrinsic — and then for constructive — reasons.

Here is another illustration. A person displays some arrogance (i.e., everything involving the ego is driven in part by egotism) by thinking well of herself and proving it by making clear that she wants others to think of her as Trustee Number One. Reaching out to be an attractive agent of trust can also be a gesture designed to win the approval of those who have not been reached out to in this way before. If these others accept the offer, the culture of trust grows. However, the involvement in truster/trustee relations can be purely selfish: that is, both sides keep their part of the bargain because both foresee profit for themselves if they keep their word. And even that approach can contribute to the complex culture of trust; by no means are all motives pure in most human relations.

Deontology and Trust: Keeping Trust as a Duty

A large area remains after one has done all the calculating of odds and risks, the writing of contracts and execution of deeds, and the express-

93

ing of self-interest and coalition for common goals that depend on trust. One might call it another horizon for those who look out and venture onto the unfamiliar terrain where trust should matter. This horizon is constituted by philosophical and religious commitments. Prime among these is *deontological ethics:* one has a duty, no matter what, to help make the world work by engaging others in bonds based on trust. Such ethics is usually seen as moving deeper than strategic and pragmatic approaches do; such ethics can be abandoned once a mission has been partly completed — or if one of the other parties grows complacent, weary, bored, or restless. If someone is moved by duty, he has made commitments, often implicit, that are firm and lasting, subject to revision — yes, but not lightly — or desertion, but only at expense of the integrity of the truster's self and his participation in a culture of trust.

Deontology addresses, but by itself does not "solve," the issue of truster-trustee risk. This came home to me one afternoon on a liberal arts college campus. I introduced my weekend host to the school's president, and I asked the standard question that, I trust, campus executives like to be asked: "What are you working on?" I knew what the school's trustees trusted him to work on: fund-raising and all that goes with it. Most campus administrators, however, like to take advantage of their intellectual environment and "stay alive" themselves, so they often work at projects they had underway before they were entrusted with leading a campus.

"Well, you know my area," the president answered. "Now I'm working on a fresh approach to deontological ethics."

"What's that?" asked my host, who is sophisticated but has had no reason to pursue excellence in Greek language studies. The president and I explained that the Greek word for "duty" was locked into that barbaric-sounding word: *de oon.* So how does that approach address ethics? Duty can just mean carrying out commands that someone else gives you so that you will get a paycheck and perhaps a corner window at the office. Now, carrying out assigned duties is certainly a matter that ethics and ethicists address. However, deontological ethics involves the will, conscience, and moral factors in the agents themselves.

"How," we were asked by the host, "does one decide what duty is, what dutiful tasks one should follow?"

"First," the president said, "you have to figure out what you think the meaning and purpose of life are. The answers to that question positions you to decide how duty calls you to address that."

The questioner went further: "How do you decide about meaning and purpose?"

"That pulls you into questions of philosophy, religion, and worldview. We'd have to discuss that at length," said the president.

And discuss it we did, at dinner tables where sixteen of us who gather for a weekend each year like to converse. Now we had a new guest, who helped everyone address the connection between duty and the meaning of life. Of course, we did not resolve anything, but we learned how deeply one must probe to find out how someone who offers trust becomes trustworthy — against all odds. For the majority of the world's populations, that deepest grounding would be in one's perception of the deepest values, which, as I have mentioned, many of them would associate with religion. But philosophy matters.

The Ethical Issues When Trust-Commitments Collide

One of the most problematic tasks in building cultures of trust is to propose what agents should do when two kinds of trust-commitments are at war in themselves or their group. The problem is most intense when it becomes clear that a person must decide which commitment to keep and thus which trust apparently to break. Philosopher Paul Ricoeur proposed — reluctantly, one must suppose — an "ethic of distress."[12] It parallels Søren Kierkegaard's "teleological suspension of the ethical."[13] Trust commitments are matters of ethics. Even the most trustworthy individuals and groups may find themselves in situations in which no action can be described as simply ethical or capable of building and holding trust among all those who are involved. To illustrate this I will introduce a case study. Before narrating it, prepare to notice that in the story the commander of a destroyer has a trust relationship with people in military service on his side, a relationship implying that he must do what he can to preserve their lives. Let Joseph Sittler pose it:

12. Paul Ricoeur, *History and Truth* (Evanston, IL: Northwestern University Press, 1965), pp. 243ff.

13. Søren Kierkegaard, *Fear and Trembling: A Dialectical Lyric,* trans. Walter Lowrie (Princeton, NJ: Princeton University Press,1945), pp. 79ff. ("Problem I: Is There a Teleological Suspension of the Ethical?").

In . . . *The Cruel Sea,* a dramatic instance . . . is presented. The commander of a destroyer, convoying a fleet of merchant ships, has finally located the submarine which had sunk several ships and caused the loss of hundreds of lives. The sonar-device which located the hidden submarine indicated that it was precisely at the point where, on the surface of the water, some hundreds of men, previously torpedoed, were swimming about. To drop a depth bomb for the destruction of the submarine would at the same time mean the destruction of the men swimming in the water. There was but an instant to make his choice, and the commander made it knowing that no choice available could be anything but death-dealing. The subsequent tormented statement of the commander, "One must do what one must do — and say one's prayers," is an eloquent condensation of the ethical situation. "One must do" — for inactivity, refusal to do anything, is already to do something. And that something is not good. . . . "What one *must* do" is not an open choice; definite alternatives are absolutely given. Both are deadly.[14]

Sittler, being a theologian, went on to rescue the situation further by the prayer reference, introducing a kind of *deus ex machina;* but that theological point does not compromise or diminish the drama of the philosophical ethical position on trust. It will often commit one to acting in pursuit of one trust-commitment but at the expense of the other. Trust talk, obviously, is often life-and-death talk. Ricoeur's ethic of distress demands that, after people have made an agonizing decision and acted on it, they must work strenuously to restore, as soon and as completely as possible, the framework in which pursuit of the ethical can again be consistent.

Trust-Building in More Prosaic Contexts

Not all philosophically based issues are as stark as this one. Cultures of trust are not based only on extremely complex ethical choices. They are built up through consistent, habitual, day-to-day engagements and policies in ordinary life. Scientists sometimes — some would say often —

14. Joseph Sittler, *The Structure of Christian Ethics* (Baton Rouge: Louisiana State University Press, 1958), pp. 82-83.

have to make crucial decisions. Most of the time, however, they have time to propose and test experiments and policies. Many of the possibilities for them to contribute to cultures of trust are to be clear of their identities, the limits and potentials of their professions, and their recognition that they must communicate with others in differing professions. The same can be said of religionists, who also regularly deal with life-and-death decisions and fateful measures, and who also need to reach out in trust and communication to others. Politicians have reason to deal with both kinds of decisions — and with still others. I will now explore trust-making and trust-breaking practices and policies in the worlds of science, religion, and public life.

CHAPTER 5

Correcting "Category Mistakes"

———◦◉◦———

I ntellectual mistrust has social and political effects.

Were scientists restricting their dismissals of religion to foot-notes in scientific journals, fellow scientists would possibly take them seriously; but, whether in agreement or disagreement with them, fellow scientists would not likely take the subject to the faculty club at lunch, to the classroom, or on the academic lecture circuit.

Were religious figures restricting their criticisms of science, at least in some of its forms, to paragraphs in theological journals, colleagues in theology and religious studies would quite possibly notice what they wrote, and then they would look up from the journal to pursue what they had been about.

Were people in public affairs, especially politicians, free to take time off from soliciting votes or passing legislation and running civil af-fairs, they would perhaps become aware of conflicts among scientists and religious thinkers, but, having little to gain by getting involved, could be expected to back off from the scene in an "I'll let you two fight it out" spirit.

If those three examples point to the outer limits of the conflicts, most people would join the "you two fight it out" bystanders who, having taken notice, would turn back to their business at computers, in text-books, or at the stadium. But the limits mentioned tend to be ignored, pushed back, or transcended, so a crisis of trust in such fields has larger consequences.

Speaking of consequences, to quote an old book title, *Ideas Have Consequences*. People with ideas often represent constituencies, and constituencies represent power, which is exemplified in public opinion polls, setting of priorities, choice of vocation, organizing higher education, establishing priorities, and much more.

Science and Religion: Their Modes and Categories

When first-rate scientists take to platforms and airwaves or write books that aspire to and sometimes achieve best-selling status in attempts to turn their mistrust into polemics, they acquire fame, notoriety, and enemies they would not have to make. Yet their polemics are only important because they represent celebrity and sensations that pass. Subtler forms of suspicion toward all things religious are apparent when some medics simply close the door whenever topics affecting the spiritual interests of patients and the public come up. Doing so consistently dampens curiosities and closes off possibilities that could mean healing. To notice this is not to suggest that medical scientists and physicians have to be theologians in disguise, aspiring experts in fields far beyond their own. It does suggest that a more holistic approach to learning and care can produce benefits, even if it means only keeping conversation going across the disciplines and vocations.

When second-rate religionists take to the same platforms or their own airwaves, or write books that attack the scientific enterprise for its godlessness or for extreme statements by some scientists, they gain attention and clienteles that serve to inhibit scientific inquiry. Several times a year legislative battles over evolution, stem-cell research, birth control, science texts, and the like gain attention nationally. These sensational cases reflect battles that go on in hundreds of local school boards, scores of state public school textbook commissions, and ethics panels in hospitals.

When first-, second-, or third-rate politicians or televised pundits become aware of the tensions that go with mistrustful scientists, religionists, and their constituencies or claques, and when they follow through by exploiting these tensions to gain votes, viewers, or followers, they complicate the efforts of scientists and religionists, who characteristically take each other seriously, give each other leeway, put the best construction on controversial endeavors and statements, and combine patience with curiosity.

Nothing that I have written in those paragraphs is designed to damper debate or inhibit argument. Science prospers as scientists subject the proposals and findings of other scientists to examination, experiment, and counterargument. Suspicion in such cases is not only to be tolerated, but the public should advocate it. When "faith healers," in the name of religion, make claims for cures that can be subjected to scrutiny based on data, and if scientists are silent under those circumstances, medical disaster can result. Religion prospers when religious figures expose those other religionists who, in the name of God, exploit people, engage in scandalous fund-raising activities, or use moral sleight-of-hand in support of their claims. The exposers are doing what religious people are supposed to do. "Test the spirits" is a biblical command that comes on the highest authority in the minds of the Christian majority.

The science/religion nexus is serving us well as a case study of the circumstances and consequences of mistrust in two of the most important zones of human life. Since the issues defined here will not be well addressed through public-relations endeavors, semantic glosses, sweet talk, or entertaining distractions, it will be profitable for us to pause and draw on resources of one philosophically minded poet and then three modern philosophers. They will help us go deeper into the question and perhaps find partially fresh addresses to relative solutions. (Modesty of claims is in order here!)

While it is, of course, not possible to inquire about or conceive of the many aspects of the relationship between science and religion, scholars have to begin somewhere. That somewhere, in my mind, is basic. It has to do with the *modes* of experience that, if not noted, can inspire mistrust. Such notice will also focus on the disparate languages that result from these and are appropriate to them. Such languages have been referred to as contributing to *universes of discourse*.

Trust begins to break down when the parties, spokespersons, and agents in these different universes make what philosophers since Aristotle have called an *ignoratio elenchi* (a "category mistake"). It represents a confusion that often appears in controversies among some kinds of scientists and religionists. Examining the consequences of such confusions or irrelevances can help produce a necessary — but, of course, by no means sufficient — address to the problems I have begun to point out. Only confusion can result when a category mistake appears. To suggest how difficult, indeed impossible, it is to respond to, refute, or affirm such a mistake is evident when it appears even in a form as simple as "Good morning, he explained."

How can there be trust when a scientist offers an "irrelevant conclusion" (one common definition for category mistakes) by applying scientific categories in attempting to prove or disprove the "truth" of any and all religious statements. Conversely, the religionist makes a category mistake when trying to render scientific any appeals to a transcendent experience or an exclusive divine revelation. Such an experience is not accessible to anyone but the person who has had the experience or to those who believe in a particular deity. Even appropriate conflict with scientists, for example, is then out of the question, since there must be some common ground behind every argument. Otherwise, what would the contestants fight over? *Ignoratio elenchi* is an argument whose premises cannot be related in any direct way to what is at issue.

It is often noted that categorical mistakes occur or result from misplaced rhetoric in attempts to persuade people, as in political argument or religious witness. High school biology teachers complain that in community meetings over the issue of what should be taught in science classrooms, fundamentalist advocates of "creation science" do not deal with scientific categories at all, or they do so with what we might call "verbal sleight-of-hand." They appeal to the religious sensibilities of people and use religious arguments that are only slightly veiled behind scientific terminology borrowed for the occasion. On the other hand, some scientific apologists "disprove" the existence of God and some of the meanings associated with metaphysics or the transcendent by subjecting to empirical tests aspects of existence that most religious people would not claim were open to scientific testing.

Ignoratio elenchi violates what would be valid in one sphere by misapplying it in another. Two Muslims can compare the term or concept of "Islam" (translated "submission") in both Shi'a and Sunni contexts. They will often disagree — perhaps vehemently and sometimes at swords' points — with each other. There would not be separate movements within Islam if the adherents to both agreed on everything. However, the two would be able to understand "where the other is coming from" and what the other is talking about. And where there is good will, there can even be a spiritual kinship. Thus Anglicans and Roman Catholics can agree on many aspects of sacramental life because they have similar concepts of the sacramental transaction. When they speak of the consecrated bread and wine on the altar as being "the body and blood of Christ," they are not making a claim that something that is going on and is recognized in the sanctuary is able to be verified empirically as the physical body of Christ. Chemically, the wine is wine and obviously not blood, and when a cynical scientist sets out to deride communicants and call them cannibals, these worshipers, including the Catholics among them, might dismiss the derisiveness as the result of a category mistake. In the face of criticism on this front, they quite literally have nothing to say in response: "ignorance of refutation" is what *ignoratio elenchi* means.

Only absurdity can come out of action scenes like the one on film in which Basil Fawlty sets out to "'punish' [his] motor-car for breaking down by flogging it with a branch."[1] He is displaying *ignoratio elenchi.* A commentator on the work of the late British philosopher Michael Oakeshott offers this illustration: "Water, to use an obvious example, has little in common with H_2O, and neither has much relation to the poetic images of water in *The Ancient Mariner.* Each mode plays by its own rules, as it were, and to mix them is like playing basketball in the middle of a game of football."[2] In his *Modes of Experience,* Oakeshott provides another illustration: "That what is arithmetically true is morally neither true nor false, but merely irrelevant, appears obvious."[3]

Oakeshott was being only somewhat hyperbolic when he called the category mistake "the most fatal of all errors," one that "occurs whenever argument or inference passes from one world of experience to another, from what is abstracted from one world of experience to another."[4] Such a mistake is so drastic, the philosopher explained, because it is necessary to recognize the differences among the modes of experience. Doing so is a human effort to resolve some of the conclusions of experience. If these modes get mixed up, only worse confusion results, as it does when a false clarity, an illusion or delusion, results. False clarity here contributes to mistrust when an agent in one "world" seeks to communicate with one in

1. I have borrowed this example from Robert Grant, in *Thinkers of Our Time: Oakeshott,* ed. Jesse Norman (London: Claridge, 1990), p. 40.

2. Kenneth Minogue, "Modes and Modesty," in Jesse Norman, ed., *The Achievement of Michael Oakeshott* (London: Duckworth, 1993), p. 46.

3. Michael Oakeshott, *Experience and Its Modes* (Cambridge: Cambridge University Press, 1933), p. 76.

4. Oakeshott, *Experience,* p. 5.

another in a form that depends on category mistakes, on which nothing can depend except Basil Fawlty's folly.

In his later work, Oakeshott spoke less of category mistakes and more of an "irrelevance" that resulted when there was such confusion. In an essay entitled "The Voice of Poetry," he accused such agents of confusion of being irrelevant. In summary, says scholarly observer Steven Anthony Gerencser, this error results "when one voice presumes to speak with authority over the concerns of all other voices, assuming its voice and idiom to be the only one with importance or meaning."[5] This particular commentator saw the source of irrelevance to be "a pointed form of confusion, *superbia,* or pride."

> [Irrelevance appears] when a voice consciously dismisses other voices, assuming that all meaning is capable of being expressed in its idiom. Such a voice either does not recognize or ignores that it, in fact, speaks in a particular idiom. It recognizes other voices — if at all — only as idiomatic, partial and incomplete. *Ignoratio elenchi* identifies a situation of confusion; *superbia* identifies a situation where confusion is sadly and dangerously compounded by arrogance.[6]

Such *superbia* is evident when, for instance, a neuroscientist who is an expert on neuron firings in the brain proposes, upon his measurement of them, a full range of moral or theological consequences, and offers a complete philosophy of life and ethics resulting therefrom. Similarly, many conservative Christians who advocate biblical "creation science" — itself a category mistake — make putatively scientific statements about the origin of the universe on the basis of their interpretation of their scripture. So would representatives of Native American religion if they used Navajo creation myths about the Grand Canyon to provide a purportedly scientific accounting of the world's genesis.

The Worlds According to Valéry, James, and Schutz

It will be difficult to reduce mistrust and to advance positive interactions between scientists and religionists without resorting to some de-

5. Steven Anthony Gerencser, *The Skeptic's Oakeshott* (New York: St. Martin's, 2000), p. 41.
6. Gerencser, *Skeptic's Oakeshott,* p. 42.

vices that will aid in an analysis of the situation. Three major thinkers can inform our study of the subject. A rather simple and focused way to begin is to conceive of someone whom we might call a "modern man," so designated by the French poet Paul Valéry. Unlike Valéry, I would argue that operating with various (often conflicting) modes is not a distinctively modern emergence. It is rather that in modernity the stimuli, the expectations, and the proximity to each other of individuals and groups with radically different experiences and worldviews are more intense than they often were in the past. So, without abandoning the recorded evidences of these modalities throughout history, I will concentrate on the one that urgently preoccupies us here.

This modern person, says Valéry, lives in a variety of practical and ideal worlds, and can negotiate his way with finesse unless he confuses the voices or categories represented in them. His existence and manner of being illustrate how an individual can entertain or be entertained by apparently contradictory modes of experience and with often isolated universes of discourse. Valéry brings him on stage in a context that merits lengthy quotation, since it illuminates the background to our inquiry concerning trust.

> Everyone today who is more or less informed of the works in critical analysis that have renewed the foundations of science, elucidates the properties of language, the origins of the forms and institutions of social life, understands that every notion, principle, or *truth,* as one used to say, is subject to review, revision, recasting; that every action is conventional, that every law, written or otherwise, is no more than approximate.
>
> Everyone tacitly agrees that the *man* in question in constitutional or civil law, the pawn in political speculations and maneuvers — the *citizen,* the *voter,* the *candidate,* the *common man,* is perhaps not quite the same as the man defined by contemporary biology, psychology, or even psychiatry. A strange contrast is the result, a curious split in our judgment. We look on the same individual as both responsible and irresponsible; we sometimes consider him irresponsible and treat him as responsible, depending on which of these fictions we adopt at the moment, whether we are in a juridical or an objective frame of mind. In the same way, we find that in many minds faith coexists with atheism, anarchy of feeling with doctrinal views. Most of us have several different opinions on the same subject, and these

may easily alternate in our judgments within a single hour, depending on the stimulus of the moment.

These are sure signs of a *critical phase* — that is, of a kind of inner disorder defined by coexisting contradictions in our ideas and inconsistencies in our actions. Our minds, then, are full of tendencies and thoughts that are unaware of each other; and if a civilization's age is to be measured by the number of contradictions it contains, by the number of incompatible customs and beliefs to be found in it, all modifying each other, or by the multiplicity of philosophies and systems of aesthetics that coexist and cohabit in the same heads, it must be agreed that our civilization is one of the most ancient. Do we not constantly find several religions, several races, several political parties represented in one family . . . and in one individual a whole armory of latent discord?

A *modern man,* and this is what makes him modern, lives on familiar terms with many contraries waiting in the penumbra of his mind and coming by turns on the stage. That is not all. We seldom notice these inner contradictions, or the coexisting antagonisms around us, and only rarely does it occur to us that they have not always been there.[7]

A second witness is the American philosopher William James, an inventor of pragmatism and a pioneer in psychological studies in the United States. Both pragmatism and psychology prepared him to speak of "attentivenesses" — Oakeshott was to call them "arrests in human experience" — and what James also calls "subuniverses." I have spoken of them here as worlds, spheres, zones, and the like. To inform our discussion of trust among scientists and religionists, we must pay close attention to "The Many Worlds," as James called them:

1. The world of sense, of physical "things"
2. The world of science, or of physical things as the learned conceive them
3. The world of ideal relations, or abstract truths believed or believable by all
4. The world of "idols of the tribe," illusions or prejudices common

7. Paul Valéry, *History and Politics* (Princeton, NJ: Princeton University Press, 1962), pp. 9-10.

to the race. All educated people recognize these as forming one subuniverse.

5. The various supernatural worlds, the Christian heaven and hell, the world of the Hindu mythology, etc. . . . Each of these is a consistent system, with definite relations among its own parts . . . (e.g., Neptune's trident has no status in Christian heaven, etc.).

6. The various worlds of individual opinion, as numerous as men are

7. The worlds of sheer madness and vagary

James adds:

> Every object we think of gets referred to one world or another of this or of some similar list. . . .[8]

It is easy to see how mistrust can grow when people make category mistakes across the boundaries of any of these seven "worlds" of William James, each of which has its place among the "regularities" and in the "assemblage" that makes up a culture of trust. Thus conceptions, semantic distinctions, languages of discourse, and the like that are appropriate to Hindu mythology may enhance life and advance the spiritual quest. But is the expert at these to be trusted as an expert on the world of physical-science entities? Of course, following Valéry, the same person can be expert in more than one, in fact, in all of these worlds, but he or she will approach them with different modes of experience and forms of discourse appropriate to each. Otherwise, only confusion and conflict will result, so distrust becomes their evident mark. The key word for James is "attentiveness":

> Propositions concerning the different worlds are made from "different points of view"; and in this more or less chaotic state the consciousness of most thinkers remains to the end. Each world *whilst it is attended to* is real after its own fashion; only the reality lapses with the attention.

And the thinker is called to sort them out, says James: "Each thinker, however, has dominant habits of attention; and these *practically elect*

---

8. William James, *Principles of Psychology* (Cambridge, MA: Harvard University Press, 1981), 2: 921-23.

from among the various worlds some one to be for him the world of ultimate realities."

The third of four witnesses to the problems resulting from category mistakes, or confusion over what James describes as "attentivenesses," is Alfred Schutz, who takes off from James and adds another term: "provinces of meaning." Any transfers of conceptions, vocabularies, and concerns from one of these to another add to confusion and potential conflict. Trusting is impossible. As in the other cases, I will quote Schutz at some length.

> The ingenious theory of William James has, of course, to be detached from its psychological setting and analyzed for its many implications. . . . We prefer to speak of finite provinces of meaning upon which we bestow the accent of reality, instead of subuniverses as does William James. By this change of terminology we emphasize that it is the meaning of our experiences, and not the ontological structure of the objects, which constitutes reality. Each province of meaning — the paramount world of real objects and events into which we can gear by our actions, the world of imaginings and phantasms, such as the play world of the child, the world of the insane, but also the world of art, the world of dreams, the world of scientific contemplation — has its particular cognitive style. It is this particular style of a set of our experiences which constitutes them as a finite province of meaning. All experiences within each of these worlds are, with respect to this cognitive style, consistent in themselves and compatible with one another (although not compatible with the meaning of everyday life). Moreover, each of these finite provinces of meaning is, among other things, characterized by a specific tension of consciousness (from full awakeness in the reality of everyday life to sleep in the world of dreams) by a specific time-perspective, by a specific form of experiencing oneself, and, finally, by a specific form of sociality.

Schutz pays respect to these various worlds of provinces of meaning:

> All these worlds — the world of dreams, of imageries and phantasms, especially the world of art, the world of religious experience, the world of scientific contemplation, the play world of the child, and the

world of the insane — are finite provinces of meaning. This means that (a) all of them have a peculiar cognitive style (although not that of the world of working with the natural attitude); (b) all experiences within each of these worlds are, with respect to this cognitive style, consistent in themselves and compatible with one another (although not compatible with the meaning of everyday life); (c) each of these finite provinces of meaning may receive a specific accent of reality (although not the reality accent of the world of working).[9]

The Modes of Michael Oakeshott

Michael Oakeshott, a modern master at discerning and dismissing category mistakes, can be most helpful to anyone who ponders the breakdown of trust when "ignorance of refutation" or "irrelevance" destroys communication. Oakeshott is helpful because he grounds his understanding in a philosophical context. In his long career he put energies into not only philosophy but also history, theories of education, and politics of a kind with which I am not in sympathy. Some saw him as the thinker behind the "Margaret Thatcher revolution" in British politics and economics. To follow up on that subject would take us beyond the scope of this chapter; here I intend to mine Oakeshott for his points about *ignoratio elenchi* as affecting science, religion, politics, and — also beyond the reach of this argument — poetry and history.

Oakeshott's earliest book, *Experience and Its Modes,* was his first elaboration of the theme. Later he concentrated more on what he called "voices of conversation" than on his original term, "the modes of experience"; yet, while there is development from one to the other, there is no contradiction. An advertiser for Oakeshott's work would be hard-pressed to make the case that this 1933 book and its concept had an immediate or large impact. When the paperback version appeared in 1985, by which time Oakeshott was being much discussed internationally, that first book about modes, published when he was only thirty-two years old, had sold fewer than one thousand copies. Oakeshott was a pioneer in linking his concept to a general idealist philosophical out-

9. Alfred Schutz, *On Phenomenology and Social Relations* (Chicago: University of Chicago Press, 1970), pp. 252, 255.

look, which one does not have to share in order to find value in his concept of "modes of experience." He acknowledged the influence of Hegel's *Phänomenology des Geistes* and Bradley's *Appearance and Reality*, which represented an outlook he felt called upon to defend in the philosophical climate of England in 1933, where and when such idealism, as he observes, had come to be "out of fashion."[10]

Two expositors of Oakeshott helpfully condense and present some basic themes related to his "modes" and "modalities." Robert Grant, in *Thinkers of Our Time: Oakeshott,* summarizes them this way: "A mode is essentially a particular, consistent way of seeing or conceiving the world, or the world as so seen, the product, roughly speaking, of a settled direction of attention."[11] This recalls William James's concept of "attentiveness." "Every idea must belong to a mode; in other words, nothing can be apprehended except under some category or other." Thus, Oakeshott argues, "an idea cannot serve two worlds."[12]

A second clarifying comment comes from Josiah Lee Auspitz, who credits the philosopher with having "left his mark on a central category: modality."

> Modal distinctions are the philosopher's way of dealing with variety without invoking facts, natural kinds, individuals or classes. One does not speak of the Golden Delicious, the Granny Smith and the McIntosh as modes of an apple, though they are varieties. But one does speak of modes of perceiving, cognizing or eating an apple, modes of being, modes of judgment, modes of the syllogism, modes of the musical scale, modes of transport and grammatical moods, a variant of modes. Modes mark the line at which judgmental distinctions are treated as differences of kind rather than degree. Modes do not take up time or space, though there may be temporal and spatial modes. Modal distinctions are compossible rather than mutually exclusive. Like the voices in Oakeshott's conversation [about which more in the next chapter] they may coexist without conflict.[13]

10. Oakeshott (in *Experience,* p. 6) mentions Bradley and Hegel; on idealism, see also p. 61.

11. Grant, *Thinkers of Our Time,* p. 38.

12. Oakeshott, *Experience,* p. 39.

13. Josiah Lee Auspitz, "Michael Oakeshott (1901-1990)," in Norman, *The Achievement,* p. 10.

Oakeshott himself condensed his view of modes for the back cover of his book: "Its theme is Modality: human experience recognized as a variety of independent, self-consistent worlds of discourse, each the invention of human intelligence, but each also to be understood as abstract and an arrest in human experience. The theme is pursued in a consideration of the practical, the historical and the scientific modes of understanding." Inside the book he says: "'Experience' stands for the concrete whole which analysis divides into 'experiencing' and 'what is experienced.'" "The world of experience is the real world; there is no reality outside experience." It is "single and whole," but "it is possible, in some measure, to break up this concrete totality," through "modification" and "arrests in human experience."

Since experience is a whole, and modes are "arrests in human experience," each mode is "defective," because it does not do justice to and cannot claim to exhaust "experience." There is, says Oakeshott, "no direct relationship between any two of these modes of experience, for each abstract world of ideas is a specific organization of the whole of experience, exclusive of every other organization. Consequently, it is impossible to pass in argument from any one of these worlds of ideas to any other without involving ourselves in a confusion . . . *ignoratio elenchi.*" Oakeshott continues: "Each mode is comprehended as a coherent, self-contained world." He isolates four modes: the scientific, the historical, the practical, and, in a later book, the poetic.[14] Of special interest here will be two, the scientific and religious experiences, though I shall briefly mention two others in order to flesh out the theme. Thus poetry's differentia is the imagination, and the artist's mode is to work *sub specie imaginationis.*

I have argued that scientific experience is distinctive. Thus, for Oakeshott, the *"scientific experience* is a single, specific mode of experience, distinguished by a single method and a single subject matter; and the world of scientific ideas is a single, homogeneous (but fortuitously divided) whole. . . . Scientific experience is defective experience: it is a mode of experience which falls short of the totality of experience, and scientific experience is abstract, conditional, incomplete, self-contained but not self-sufficient. . . ." Oakeshott points to the main feature of the *scientific mode:* "Science is the world *sub specie quantitatis;*

14. These discussions are in Oakeshott, *Experience,* pp. 9, 70, 71, 75, 76.

its differentia is the attempt to organize the world of experience as a system of measurements."[15] In this understanding, the "defective experience" in the scientific mode differs from — one can almost say is irrelevant to — the modes of poetry, history, and here, most emphatically, the practical, which includes religion.

As for the practical, in this mode "a coherent world of experience is achieved by means of action, by the introduction of actual change into existence. And the aspect of mind involved is the will. Practice is the exercise of the will; practical thought is volition; practical experience is the world *sub specie voluntatis* . . . [also *sub specie moris*]."[16] Once again, the philosopher is pointed and succinct when discussing the *practical mode:* "Practice is the world *sub specie voluntatis,* the world as a system of acts, each modifying 'what is' so as to bring it into harmony with what ought to be." The differentia relates to the implication of a "felt discrepancy between 'what is' and what we desire shall be, [and] implies the idea of 'to be' which is 'not yet.'"

Practical experience is the mode that involves "a life directed by an idea of fact, of system and of coherence," an "attempt to alter 'what is here and now' so as to agree with 'what ought to be.'" Like the scientific experience, it is also an "arrest in experience" and is therefore also defective.

Not everyone who is religious would welcome being perceived in the "practical" mode, but there are good reasons for discerning the presences and phenomena of religion there. I am an historian of religion and of Christianity, and when working as an historian, I am using the historical mode. Oakeshott summarizes it this way: "History is the world *sub specie praeteritorum* . . . : its differentia is the attempt to organize the whole world of experience in the form of the past."[17] This means that I have nothing to talk about except when something has happened, which means in the past. If people ask me to use my historical knowledge to project into the future, the universe of discourse changes, and I have nothing to be attentive to, as an historian, until something has occurred.

15. Oakeshott, *Experience,* p. 243. R. G. Collingwood condensed this mode in *The Cambridge Mind: Ninety Years of the Cambridge Review 1879-1969* (London: Jonathan Cape, 1969), p. 133.

16. For elaborations on "the practical mode," see Oakeshott, *Experience,* pp. 256-57, 259, 309-10.

17. For elaborations on "the historical mode," see Oakeshott, *Experience,* pp. 87-88, 111, 127.

I may be a hymn writer or poet in the service of the church, but as such an artist, I will be using the perceptions and vocabulary of the poet (Oakeshott's inclusive term for everyone in poetry and the visual arts). I may be a sociologist who specializes in churchly behaviors, but when dealing with my social science, I am in the scientific mode, which means to Oakeshott that I live with measurement. My social science may tell me that I am surrounded in church by people who violate church canons with respect to their sexuality. But if and when I want to make an issue of it in church life, I move from the scientific to the practical mode.

Once again, on first hearing this, many religionists would find it limiting to be discerned through the practical mode. Even more precisely, Oakeshott says that in the practical mode we see religion under the aspect of the will or the moral factor, *sub specie voluntatis* or *moris*. Various Christian theologies — and others as well, for all I know — have intense arguments about the place of the will. Is it "bound" or "free," as Luther and Erasmus debated it? No theological issues are implied here; rather, this has to do with aspects of human experience. Similarly, there are huge debates in the religions about the source, origin, expression, limits, and possibilities of the moral element or quest. For the modal thinker, none of these matters directly. The practical religious impulse is located in some moral dimension of the human, however that is discerned or explained. One can live by grace and the free, spontaneous, unmotivated love of God; yet categorically, in the language and experience of the modes, the human moral feature is what provides the vocabulary, the universe of discourse. Science can provide data about the make-up of the human, but the religious response relates to a different category.

Should my social science measurements tell me that the largest percentage of American Catholic women are practicing methods of birth control disallowed by the church, I might feel impelled to run to the Vatican and say, "Look at the statistics. You must adapt and change church teaching!" The answer I would hear first would be something revealing the sadness of the pope or Vatican scholars and officers; but these leaders would say that decisions about such practices belong to the practical — which includes the religious — mode. The statistical findings can at most serve to alert us that the Catholic leaders might rethink their stance. If they were to respond, however, it would not be a social scientific adjustment but one dealing with theology and ethics — which are in the practical mode. Here it becomes very clear that the scientific and the religious are independent of each other.

In the end, Oakeshott conceived of religion in positive ways in the practical mode.

> Religion . . . is practical experience pressed to its conclusion; in it all subordinate attempts to establish the harmony, unity or coherence of the world of practical experience — attempts such as politics and morality constitute — are swallowed up and superseded. Religious truths are those which attempt to satisfy the further claims and the largest needs of practical life. . . . If religion has anything to do with the conduct of life, then the ideas of religion — ideas such as those of deity, of salvation and of immortality — are practical ideas and belong to the world of practice. And an idea which serves this world can serve no other.[18]

Emphatically, no one is "confined" to a particular mode, as if it were a disciplined academic specialty. Like Valéry's "modern man," who can be using any one of these modes simultaneously and in turn, depending on the angle of vision, his role at the moment, our perception of him, and our distinctive language about him, the religious person can be at home with the scientist, and vice versa. More important, in Oakeshott's mind, one does not have to *be* religious to deal with the religious universe of discourse, nor *be* a scientist for the scientific mode. He speaks critically of those who do the confining. In *Modes of Experience,* he says:

> Religion, it is said, can be understood only by the religious man; science by the scientist, art by the artist and history by the historian. It is, nevertheless, wholly misleading. . . . We may leave religious questions to religious men, the problems of science to the scientist, history to the historian; it is the business of each of these to organize and make coherent his own world of experience; but to suppose that the nature of history is an historical question, or that the character of religion is a question upon which a religious man, as such, is specially qualified to advise us, would involve (to say the least) unwarranted assumptions about the character of these worlds.[19]

18. Michael Oakeshott, *Modes of Experience* (London: Methuen, 1962), p. 309.
19. Oakeshott, *Modes of Experience,* pp. 87-88.

Modes Are Not Compartments in the Mind

To some, it may seem that the approach through modes would mean compartmentalizing the spheres of "science" away from "religion." Compartmentalization implies a divorcing from the concept that experience is a whole, to be apprehended through "arrests in experience," which means through the modes. The modal approach is radically different from boxes-in-the-brain compartmentalization. This will become clear as we address a problem left by this study of the experience and the modes. How do people avoid solipsism? How can we keep professionals in various fields using different modes from sequestering themselves in echo chambers, talking only to themselves? Oakeshott was aware of that problem, and we can pursue our inquiry through his categories and strategies. What he latterly posed to deal with this was a combination of "voices" where "modes" had been, and "conversation," which he elaborated on as a construct and instrument. It is the creative alternative to misconceived compartmentalization, and it merits detailed treatment.

CHAPTER 6

Conversation and "What It Means to Be Human"

————◦⟨◉⟩◦————

"**A** scientist, a priest, an historian, and a poet walk into a bar. . . ." The line sounds like a lead-in to a tired joke. Let the four of them, instead, here be representatives, in their disciplined and professional lives, of four of the "modes of experience" or "distinctive voices" that can easily enough engage in Conversation A. This means that they could trust each other to have little difficulty discussing common interests such as professional football, the price of gasoline, the quality of the drink, or the weather — the topics of Conversation A. They would not be talking *as* scientist, priest, historian, or poet in any formal or defining sense, though they and others in the bar could be aware of their identities and vocations. The special color they would bring to their conversational roles would likely have to do with their shared or antagonistic alma maters, such as the University of Southern California, which helped produce the scientist, and the University of Notre Dame, where the priest did his preseminary college work. The historian and the poet may have been in the same college fraternity together, or they simply both appreciate Impressionistic art. They can trust each other easily, as far as that goes, meaning that the trust has to last only as long as it takes to drink a mug of Guinness stout or a margarita. Their hour in the bar may be a wonderfully humanizing event, well earned by each member of the overworked quartet.

The scientist, priest, historian, and poet could also enter a bar and take up any number of topics that would make up Conversation B. This conversation might easily metamorphose into argument and threaten to bring about the end of their discourse. The scientist at this hypothetical watering hole near a campus is poised to argue that a "God gene" or some other mechanism with the neuron firings in the brain produced mystical states and, *voila!* he thus includes in the bargain the idea of God dissolving during a routine brain scan. The priest thinks that what he has heard from the scientist is a reductionist measuring of neurons, which leaves all religious expression "nothing but" something material. For him, such measuring does not do justice to the fact that, in the circles of mystics, certain adepts might witness to the fact that they have been absorbed by the One, the All, God. Both scientist and priest then ask the historian what she thinks of the future of this subject: Will materialist reductionism or spiritual transcendence have the greater appeal a century from now? She replies that, while it is fun to write scenarios, place bets, or make up games about the future, *as* a specialized scholar, she has nothing in her historian's toolbox to help her come up with anything to say. The poet — in this case someone who would put her imagination to work — points out that the four interlocutors taken together would make good characters in a theater-of-the-absurd drama, be it a tragedy or a comedy, about how no one understands anyone anymore.

The scientist in such a circumstance could well debate another scientist or a dedicated amateur in matters of the laboratory or clinic. A Catholic priest could argue with an Orthodox priest about how differently churches East and West are interpreting their respective traditions. A historian could discuss the fine points of interpretation about the schism of "1054 and All That," or about popular history versus old-school, high-culture history. And the playwright-poet could trust another person in the world of theater to chat about the makings of a technically fine play. Would the four of them, on any professional and technical level, be able to understand the thought-world, language, and modes of experience of the others if they confined their approach to their discipline's mode or voice? Would they want to? Do they have the motivation to do more than show mere courtesy, fall into boredom, or sneer at each other (over a second drink) because the other three do not give the same priority or comprehension to something they consider vital to the republic? Would the conversation break up with one or another complaining to the other three, "I just can't conceive of where you're coming from." (Perhaps the poet, as literary artist, would point out that the others were ending their sentences of complaint with a preposition, but otherwise the plot would advance along predictable lines.)

We would have here a representation not of four personalities and personality types, four regional backgrounds, four levels of learning — nor of four people who could not stand each other. They might, for the sake of the story, bring good will and a spirit of tolerance to the venture and let the drinks they consume mellow them. Yet the "modes of their experience" are distinctive: in Oakeshott's phrase, they speak with "distinctive voices." Since each inhabits a distinct province of meaning — if each one stays within the world to which he or she is attentive — each person would make it difficult to know the others, or to care to know them. They would need some instrument or structure to help them handle their disparate universes of discourse. Communicating with each other would be good for the republic. To be unable, unwilling, or unready to do so would cheat other congenial bar patrons who would be listening in, and it would cut off "the real world" inhabited by the ordinary — or at least the different — people around them.

Michael Oakeshott provides the summary of such occasions when he speaks of a culture in these terms: "[T]he identity of a culture . . . remains obscure until we have some conception of the relationship of its components." Each of these components "constitutes the terms of a distinct, conditional understanding of the world and a similarly distinct idiom of human self-understanding. "Their differences and distinctions are valuable and their differences are intrinsic." Notice also that "each is secure in its autonomy so long as it knows and remains faithful to itself." It is important to observe about the four that "they are not inherently contentious and they are incapable of refuting one another."[1] So they cannot debate well. But they *can* converse, since conversation is a very distinct mode of discourse, a mode that is decisive for any people who would build cultures of trust.

In our imaginary visit to their chosen bar, we can more formally consider how the four characters might begin to relate to each other in what I have called Conversation B, the substantive one. This means examining their worldviews and then working to build trust. It should be clear that mistrust does not ordinarily result from chattered snippets, casual comments, media epigrams, or poetry slams. No, again quoting Michael Oakeshott (whose ghost is at the edge of this encounter, look-

1. Michael Oakeshott, *The Voice of Liberal Learning,* ed. Timothy Fuller (New Haven: Yale University Press, 1989), p. 38.

ing on from its place along the bar), they instead represent "beliefs, perceptions, ideas, sentiments and engagements" that are of vital importance but can remain barriers to trust. Trust grows when the "variety of distinct languages of understanding" are recognized as such and are approached through the invitation from the others to converse. Trust cannot thrive where participants must make category mistakes and become incomprehensible or off-putting to the others. The conversation would stall or end if one of the parties experienced the exchange as hierarchical. In such a case, a dominant member of the quartet would argue that one mode alone could bear the weight of all inquiry and conversation on a given topic or a whole field of human concern.

When we leave behind this fictional gathering, as we must, there remain pointed questions bidding for attention. How might a public find bases for beginning to build trust and move toward understanding among scientists and religionists, since these two live in different worlds? And how might we understand these worlds of people whose thought patterns and discourse are appropriate to one or another of their "arrests in experience," since their "modes" cannot translate to those of others? We can begin responding to such questions by noting that the same person can operate on some level with all the modes, be they poetic, scientific, historic, philosophical, religious, political, or practical. The same person can also, at any time, draw on a particular mode and appropriate something of the experience of others. They need some instrument for inaugurating and furthering communication.

Provinces of Meaning

To speak, as I have, of a string of concepts such as "provinces of meaning," "worlds" to which one is "attentive," "modes of experience," and "universes of discourse" may contribute to our understanding of why trust is often broken down across the barriers — or was never established in the first place. I have made a case study of two such provinces, modes, or universes: *science* and the complex communities of scientists, on the one hand, and *religion* and the expansive community of religionists, on the other, though politics or poetry could have served as well to illustrate the point.

Temptations to succumb to frustration are abundant. Thus, breaking off the dialogue and leaving everyone isolated in enclaves would be unfaithful to endeavors that bring promise for the larger communities and societies. In response, I begin by noting that a disruption of dialogue would be unrealistic because it is obvious that communication *does* exist on many levels. In common and ordinary life, biologists and deacons can — and often do — understand aspects of each other's world. Some scientists may be better read in theology than many deacons, and some deacons keep up on sciences enough to be able to discern what their scientist friends are talking about.

Numerous agencies and study centers that have been founded to bring together at least some dimensions of science and religion, as well as academic programs devoted to bridging gaps among scientists and thinkers in the fields of religion, do thrive and offer promise. Not recognizing such approaches and achievements would represent bad reporting, bad grace, and bad faith. It is helpful and useful to track them and observe how both leaders and "ordinary people" in their programs do the bridging and how they can work in common.

If it is an ethical call to be realistic and accurate when observing and reporting, it is also an ethical call of serious people to be faithful to the positive intentions of others. Those others are not content to be confined within their discipline or to be walled off from everyone else. Rejecting them would be unfaithful to the record of those who contribute to research, healing, building bridges, and engaging in the politics of the academy, foundations, and common civil life. Not encouraging further exploration across boundaries would also create problems. Therefore, in due course, after setting out to advance communication, I will attempt such reporting.

Whoever has isolated one of the modes of experience can easily recognize how impossible it would be to live a full human life within only one of the provinces of meaning. It would be foolish to settle for a single mode of experience or to believe that one has exhausted learning by remaining content with an isolated universe of discourse. I will illustrate by referring to my two chosen worlds: science and religion. We can imagine what life and learning would be like if there had never been and were not now communication across the zones. One can also illustrate this by negative reference: there are scientists who believe that nothing to which religion points can have a positive potential. There are also religionists who contend that science has only negative potentials in the zones of life in which religion appears to be relevant. Neither of these helps advance cultures of trust.

Since our characters were described as inhabiting different "provinces of meaning," we need to examine that technical term. "Province" is, of course, a spatial term, applied metaphorically to various approaches; "meaning" can refer to the whole range of goals that humans seek with head and heart, the intellect and the passions. The French phenomenologist Maurice Merleau-Ponty put it well when he said, "Because we are present to a world, we are condemned to meaning."[2] A "world" here refers to the whole physical, intellectual, and spiritual environment of which Ortega spoke when defining culture. A person who has developed in any particular environment did not elect to be conceived and born. She did not get to choose her parents or the genetic package — the DNA complex — with which she comes from the womb. Yet, even before conscious thought processes are discernible, she finds and suckles her mother's breast, and, though the reference may seem a bit oblique, she finds meaning in that suckling. She may well unconsciously carry through her life both positive and negative aspects of that. She may trust instinctively, or she may have difficulty trusting.

The infant grows and is then occupied with a search for meaning that does not end even if and when she reaches her ninetieth year. By then experience, memory, critical thinking, and the making of choices will have contributed to meaning and encouraged — yes, further necessitated — the pursuit of meaning. The goatherd in Azerbaijan is as engaged in his projects as is the logical positivist philosopher at Oxford. While the philosopher may be well-read, much traveled, and surrounded by human "others," finitude forces limits on anyone who pursues meaning: that is, she cannot be or have been everywhere, or have come to know everything in every way. Lifelong, the search for meaning gets focused in the sensibility and vocation of each person.

The phrase Alfred Schutz used for this, as we have read, was "provinces of meaning." This phrase, among other things, can refer to the boundaries of an academic discipline. Being an astrophysicist inspires certain curiosities and calls for kinds of intellectual endeavors that differ from those involved in becoming an imam or a priest. What counts as evidence in one province is discounted in another. Once more we must speak of *ignoratio elenchi,* making "category mistakes," which occur when one has not learned the rules of the game in particular prov-

---

2. Huston Smith made this phrase into a book title: *Condemned to Meaning* (New York: Harper and Row, 1962).

inces and violates boundaries with others. To return to the physical and geographical references: mastering the techniques of mountaineering, for example, which enables one to scale frigid and snowy peaks, does not prepare one to talk to — or even make sense to — anyone who is preparing to traverse sere and barren deserts. Learning to tend to grazing animals across vast prairies does little to help one nurse flowers in a tiny window box. One can find meaning in climbing mountains, exploring deserts, minding flocks, and encouraging flowers to grow outside the window, but different kinds of meaning are determinative.

The anthropologist who engages in participant-observation at weddings in Turkmenistan has entered a different province than is his when he, his bride, and their families plan a wedding of their own on Park Avenue in New York — or when the bridal couple makes love on the honeymoon. The priest who ministers to a cancer-ridden patient or an off-duty oncologist enters a different province of meaning than either of them inhabits when he learns that he himself has cancer, and that he must summon resources to face it existentially. The province of the researcher differs from the province dwelt in by those he or she studies.

It is possible to find people who, having chosen to live in a single province of meaning, subsequently do all they can to distance themselves from those who are at home in other provinces. Thus a cloistered nun can become extremely competent at chanting the biblical Psalms every day; and, to add quality to her specialty, having taken a vow of silence, she may refuse to participate in discourse of any kind. She is forbidden by her own original choice to chat with a fellow nun, to intone words at all except in chanted prayer, ever to leave the four walls of the monastery, ever to be seen except behind the veil she wears and draws shut to exclude others. Yet, even in the most extreme circumstances, total intellectual and spiritual hermitage is impossible. The hermit monk has to "come down" from his pursuit of The All and be subjected to something alien when he has a CAT scan or an X-ray administered by people who for their purpose live in different provinces of meaning.

I have been amused to read brochures prepared by modern public relations and advertising firms that beckon one to visit, typically, an Amish community that has set out, ordinarily amiably, to keep non-Amish religious provinces of meaning at a distance. An advertising brochure will say honestly — remember, the Amish community is known for virtues of truth-telling — that one can find peace by visiting such a community for a weekend. The beds will be clean, the food superb, and the opportunity for contemplation, self-assessment, or "conversing" in silence with God commendable. Those who accept the offer to visit will have to obey this set of commands: leave your cell phones, radios, and portable televisions behind; take care not to bump into a horse-and-buggy; and abandon your car in a remote parking lot at the edge of the community. On the last page of the brochure there follows a rationale: our community, it explains, is a two-centuries-old commune of people who would serve God by cutting off communication with the larger world. This decision amounts to withdrawing from the world of those effects that keep the rest of us preoccupied. After all this printed counsel there is one more line: "And if you'd like to learn more, contact www.amishvillages.org."

Such a slight tale becomes a fable suggesting that provinces of meaning intersect, impinge on each other, and interrupt continuity in another. Observing how people negotiate among these provinces, noticing whether and how they do this elegantly or with consistency, can encourage more people to risk building communities of trust, in which more complex levels of communication are to occur. That they do occur is because humans are social beings. *How* they occur is a question that deserves inquiry.

Attentiveness to "Worlds," "Modes," and "Voices"

What I have sought to portray by referring to Alfred Schutz and his "provinces of meaning" is enlarged by reference to what I also noted earlier but must now revisit in William James, when he speaks of "worlds" to which one is and must be "attentive." A person cannot be equally attentive to them all at all times and with the same degree of engagement and expertise with respect to each. The languages and approaches to them differ from each other in kind. Each person acquires some skills and curiosities that prepare her for being attentive and thus contributing to the search for meaning. One may devote her childhood years to music and the pursuit of a musical career, and that endeavor may introduce her to a world of schools, master classes, competitions, agents, appearances, reviews, quests for recognition and status, and enjoyment. She learns theory and hears or makes sounds in one key or another, on one instrument or another. She creates and responds to a "world" or set of worlds that are not merely fired at her point-blank, as it were, but discovered, explored, and developed.

This musical expert may enjoy attending tennis matches. She watches television, reads the newspapers and tennis magazines, hangs out with her sister, who is a tennis star — but she cannot wield a racket. The walls of her tennis-playing sister's bedroom reveal that the latter is attentive to a world different from the musician's. Posters of champions cling to the walls; some how-to books crowd others off the shelf; trophies on her vanity table give evidence of her mastery of techniques and strategy. Read her a review of a string quartet and she may be bored, or show her a report on a cricket match and she will be apathetic or nonresponsive: those things represent worlds to which she is not attentive. Yet she and her sister may communicate well about their Catholicism, their extended family, menus and memories, explorations of citizenship, and philanthropy. They may have become alert to criteria of excellence in many fields and find analogies and overlappings among them. Yet they can together be formally attentive within a relatively small zone of human experience and endeavor. How, then, is communication possible?

A third way of assessing experiences and manifesting them relates to what I have also explored at some length. This is the approach of Oakeshott, with his "arrests in human experience," "zones," or "voices," themes we can profitably revisit in this new context. On one level, Oakeshott is a most curiosity-stricken, polymathic philosopher; on other levels, he sounds most "provincial" about provinces of meaning, most attentive to precise and, in their own way, narrow and constrictive worlds. As we recall, he was an idealist philosopher who posited what by various empirical means can be recognized. This was his observation: for each human, "experience is a whole," but one cannot deal with all of it in even terms. There are and have to be what he called "arrests in human experience." Must one remain isolated in each?

These modes or voices imply specific categories of meaning, special languages that cannot carry over from one to the other, as Oakeshott argued and I have noted. To neglect such specialties will doom one to make category mistakes and thus frustrate communication. Indeed, doing so would render attempts to communicate truthfully and meaningfully impossible. In our sampling of the modes, which theoretically can be very numerous, we have concentrated on science and religion. Recall that the differentia of science is "measurement": hence one sees and expounds reality *sub specie quantitatis*. The differentia of religion is an attempt to alter the world, having explored it *sub specie voluntatis* or *moris* (i.e., the will or the moral framework and interest). How can we make social, cultural, and intersubjective use of these explorations unless those who deal with religion or who "are" religious can somehow communicate by translation, as it were, with others whose outlook and approach is, say, scientific or historical or poetic?

Poet Paul Valéry opened the poetic mode, and from that opening I have drawn occasion to comment on "universes of discourse," a term that has become common in modern philosophical and communication theory. The artist, novelist, or poet works with what Oakeshott called the "poetic" mode, and its differentia is the imagination. Working *sub specie imaginationis,* the poet need not do what the historian must do, which is to wait for something to happen, a happening that leaves traces out of which an historian fashions history. The poet can imagine the future. When the historian does so, she has left history behind. The poet need not worry about whether the potions about which she writes when engaged in fantasy or being fanciful work out accurately in the laboratory. The poet concocts, but she is not interested in using weights or measure and will not call it a province of science. The empirical may even represent the very province of meaning, the word to which she is attentive, the poetic mode, as being inimical to her poetic endeavor. Once again, how can there be conversation and concern for the common good, as well as the development of cultures of trust?

Yet in the common and complex human ventures, some forms of communication do occur. The mathematical scientist sees beauty in the formulas, the historian draws on the poetry and art of the past to describe a bygone age, the religionist learns rhetoric from the poet and uses it to help alter the world, as religionists in their proper concerns set out to do. As before, some common interests and competences make communication possible and do license common endeavors. What we have been describing are not "compartments," nor have we indulged in compartmentalization when dealing with modes, provinces, worlds, or universes. Often when one hears someone described as a "fundamentalist scientist," he is seen as a "compartmentalizer," one who can put the concerns of evolutionary science into one box as he witnesses "scientifically" to a young earth, a six-day creation in which natural selection does not count and the origin of species is explained apart from biblical revelation. How does he do that? By placing everything about one in a compartment and then not letting what is in one compartment contaminate what is in the other.

Conversation as the Means of Access

The beginning point for building trust across the boundaries of special-ization, across the separation of modes, or over the confusion of voices — such as those uttered by scientists, religionists, or others represent-ing one or another of the "arrests of experience" — is conversation. In what follows I will outline some specifics that go with the appeal for con-versing, as well as for both understanding and nurturing conversation.

Conversation is, of course, not the be-all and end-all of trust-building; but without it there can only be soliloquy, solipsism, isolation, distortion, or misrepresentation. When a person bids for conversation by opening one, she makes possible the chance for her conversation partner to impart something of her soul, herself, and her ideas and com-mitments. To analyze how this can be, we start with some definitions of conversation and follow them with explorations by various philosophers — or poets — about its art and its role. The prime and primary access to this universe of discourse is, of course, the dictionary, especially one that operates on "historical principles," namely through the mode or voice that works with the past. The classic if complex clarifier here is *The Oxford English Dictionary on Historical Principles*.

In the definition of "conversation" in this dictionary, the first two references are to obsolete but very informative usages. They have to do with communication across provinces of meaning, to show attentive-ness to worlds, illustrate modes of experience, and suggest universes not of discourse but of ways of life. "Conversation" is, among other things, "the action of consorting or having dealings with others; being together; commerce, intercourse, society, intimacy," all of which mean-ings are regrettably marked *obs.* Why do I say regrettably? Because lead-ers or experts in the various universes of discourse often do not consort with each other. The priest is welcomed at bedside but not in the sur-geons' conclave, though both priest and surgeon are involved with the same "other," who may need the services of both of them. I am not sen-timentalizing the potential of conversation between them, or setting out to complicate the lives of busy people by portraying that profession-als need to chatter with or pester each other. Here we are talking in the mode that the dictionary signals with *fig.* ("figuratively"), which repre-sents the kind of discourse that proceeds on some occasions at certain levels with the needs of the patient in view.

The key for us is the definition itself, which is: "To convey the thoughts reciprocally in talk . . . to engage in conversation; to talk *with* (a person) *on, upon* (a subject); *in* (a language, voice)." And now the dictionary allows for a sigh of relief on the part of the user when it concludes that this is "the ordinary current sense." Here we return once again to Michael Oakeshott and his concern for avoiding category mistakes. Strangers almost naturally and inevitably have difficulty trusting each other. Does the stranger in a foreign city who offers me his services as a guide merit confidence, or do I keep up my sense of suspicion because he may lead me into a trap? Is the alien trustworthy among citizens whose common interests have been long tested in their conversation with each other? No one pretends that conversation is a foolproof interpersonal protective shield. Few depict conversation as a license for every kind of risk or all displays of confidence. The proverbial "con man" has mastered the language of the tribe he is invading even before he invades. He may be cunning, deceptive, beguiling, manipulative, and hard to size up. Yet, for all the hazards, awareness of him dare not block out all possibilities. Somewhere there has to be a beginning for builders of trust. Somehow barriers between the self and the other have to be broken down if there is to be any confidence.

In true conversation, one listens (picture the scientist hearing the religionist) just as one speaks (imagine the same scientist doing the talking as the religionist listens); in that interchange, ideas flow and confidence has a chance to build. If conversation involves one partner always having to await time to speak, bursting unbidden on the speech of someone else, then true conversation is not occurring and cannot occur. The fundamentalist in religion or in science has no patience for hearing the other and has the impulse only to denounce the other. However, the "other," in the act of conversing, wants to inform and educate him- or herself. The good conversationalist helps the other organize and assess reality. He may often include invitations in conversation: bids to have the other join him and his friends in designated places. Conversations, as everyone knows, go on at all levels, whether about grocery lists, the prospect of removing a wisdom tooth, facing prostate cancer, batting averages, or the ordination of homosexuals to the clergy.

At its best, such conversation can move the partners to frontiers of fancy or can inspire them to write agendas and scenarios that can lead to daring activities for which the partners were readied by their long conversation. Sometimes a group is moved to common action after a figurative "light has been turned on," thanks to discourse. If there is to be trust, participants have to develop an ethic and a ready ear. They can be motivated to both of those by conversation as they might not have been through argument and debate. Conversation allows the other to make unanticipated resolves because resolves are based on ideas that did not spring forth when one of the partners had been isolated. It also allows for mutual criticism of a kind that argument cannot easily elicit, because argument produces triumphant winners and browbeaten losers. In our time, conversation enabled by electronic communication can achieve much. Think of lovers who use a cell phone to define themselves after they have been confused by a partner's silence, or their writing to each other has been obscure. Friends converse to reinforce each other in their signs of affection or their questions about direction. So do specialists in one form of discourse or another.

Here is where trust comes in most boldly. A compliment from a passing stranger occasions mistrust: Is she trying to sell me something when she engages in flattering conversation? An office conversation with a competitor from without or within a company, someone who wants my place, is less fruitful for assessing motives and for sizing up the other than is conversation over dinner. Conversation in the sense of the turning in a way of life may be accompanied by revealing moves in body language, moves that cannot occur innocently or creatively among debaters. Apparently, trivial conversation about ephemeral subjects, wherein participants evaluate the other's likes and dislikes, clears the ground for advancing trust. Formal, often propagandistic, communication cannot do that as well, because the aggression of one arguer and the defenses of the other block understanding.

In "conversing" with Michael Oakeshott, we can see how conversation represented a transition from the isolating "modes of experience" to efforts at promoting the common good, and one can fill in the blanks and make connections. In a collection of Oakeshott's papers, editor Timothy Fuller has gathered many essays that focus on conversation.[3] Fuller enters forcefully into the conversation with a (warranted) polemical comment about the misuse of many discourses in contemporary higher education: that is, what is intended to build trust in such cases turns out to lead to mistrust or frustration. While criticizing E. D. Hirsch, the advocate of "cultural literacy" and the proponent of a set of

---

3. Oakeshott, *The Voice of Liberal Learning*, pp. 5, 7, 11, 13f.

materials that he thinks the culturally literate should know in order to be responsible citizens and pursuers of the common good, Fuller, in the spirit of Oakeshott, shows how contemporary education may set up occasions for mistrust:

> Contemporary education is hard-pressed to distinguish formality and civility — the general rules of "conversation" — from manipulative managerial techniques which are designed to achieve goals of apparent specificity such as "cultural literacy." The project is to harness technique to an array of cultural artefacts [sic], justified by reference to a certain conception of social improvement. . . . This approach lends itself particularly well to rhetorically powerful formulations by governmental agencies, promoting the prospect of solving educational "problems" by "educational policies."

Fuller notes that Oakeshott set forth the program of conversation because he "argued for the radical unity of human experience in thought," as we have seen in *Experience and Its Modes.* Fuller contends further that, for Oakeshott, "the relation between oneself and others is one of tension in search of reconciliation, incoherency in quest of coherency." That quest is pursued by conversation with the other, as, in our case, between the scientist and religionist. Take the issue of dealing with "nature." Recalling the modes of experience, Fuller notes that "the engagements of the contemplative, the poet, the philosopher, the scientist who seeks to understand nature's structure, the historian who is in love with the past for its own sake, *are not marginal but crucial in appreciating what it means to be human"* [emphasis added].

If we picture the scientist and the religionist seeking to converse enough that they can move from the marginal to the crucial as they try to discern what it means to be human, we have to know the limits of the venture. Conversing will not prove or disprove the existence of God in such a way that scientists as scientists would recognize it; nor would doing so confirm scientific methods or approaches or world views as final and absolute. In fact, conversation may sometimes do more to erode "certainties" than argument may. Oakeshott's key text on this theme sheds light on the issue of limits:

> In conversation, "facts" appear only to be resolved once more into the possibilities from which they were made; "certainties" are shown

to be combustible, not by being brought into contact with other "certainties" or with doubts, but by being kindled by the presence of ideas of another order; approximations are revealed between notions normally remote from one another. Thoughts of different species take wing and play round one another, responding to each other's movements and provoking one another to fresh exertions. Nobody asks where they have come from or on what authority they are present; nobody cares what will become of them when they have played their part. There is no symposiarch or arbiter; not even a doorkeeper to examine credentials. Every entrant is taken at its face-value and everything is permitted which can get itself accepted into the flow of speculation. And voices which speak in conversation do not compose a hierarchy. Conversation is not an enterprise designed to yield an extrinsic profit, a contest where a winner gets a prize nor is it an activity of exegesis. It is an unrehearsed intellectual adventure. It is with conversation as with gambling, its significance lies neither in winning nor in losing, but in wagering.

Editor Fuller draws an illuminating comparison between Oakeshott and Hobbes, one that illuminates some searches for means to bring specialists together. "Like Hobbes, Oakeshott couples a constant remembrance of the reasons for mankind to be humble, rather than proud, with a striking belief in the capacity of men so intrusted to create a world for themselves in which there is much to delight in. . . ." Oakeshott states his own case and offers aid as we seek to pursue and develop conversation as a basis for trust.

> Perhaps we may think of . . . components of a culture as voices, each the expression of a distinct and conditional understanding of the world and a distinct idiom of human self-understanding, and of the culture itself as these voices joined, as such voices could only be joined, in a conversation — an endless unrehearsed intellectual adventure in which, in imagination, we enter into a variety of modes of understanding the world and ourselves and are not disconcerted by the differences or dismayed by the inconclusiveness of it all. And perhaps we may recognize liberal learning as, above all else, an education in imagination, an initiation into the art of this conversation in which we learn to recognize the voices, to distinguish their different modes of utterance, to acquire the intellectual and moral habits ap-

propriate to this conversational relationship and thus to make our *début dans la vie humaine.*

Looking back on his own liberal education, with all its assets and liabilities, Oakeshott assessed that it prospered best when it stimulated conversation and did not always find itself converted into argument. He illustrated that with a "for instance" that is a perfect match for the major case study in this book. He said that his education was "a conversation in which each student had a distinctive voice — a conversation which occasionally degenerated into an argument (for example, *between 'science' and 'religion'*), but which in the main retained its proper character" [emphasis added]. Putting "science" and "religion" in quotation marks may have been Oakeshott's way of showing that he assumed that category mistakes in these areas have led to more confusion and disruption than in many others.

It would insult the intelligence of the reader for me to take from this the claim that the university has no place for argument. That notion would be absurd on the face of it. The public seeks and needs and demands argument in philosophy classrooms, the law school, and certainly among scientists as they test propositions, analyze malignant cells, and contend with each other over proposed "cures." Similarly, there is place for argumentation among religionists as they debate the ethics of business or war — as these are informed by religion. There can be argumentation among Catholic theologians about the meaning of texts that both sides agree are somehow authoritative. This is where the "distinctive voices" speak to — and their owners hear — those whose zones of experience and patterns of discourse do not match.

Following up on the argument between "science" and "religion," as Oakeshott poses it, one can see light thrown on contemporary arguments; even better, one can see missed communications because of category mistakes. What could be and sometimes is a promising interchange about the human condition among these "distinctive voices" has in many cases degenerated into futile arguments that soon descend to the level of shouting matches and sneering. Usually singled out on this front are the religious fundamentalists, who make category mistakes especially when they propose that their sacred texts can and must serve as scientific texts. The most hoary and over-discussed conflict on this front is the one resulting from fundamentalists (or "creationists") who argue that the world was created in six days. They know this because they use their favored text, written for other than scientific text-book purposes, to provide a scientific account. So familiar is this "creationist" approach (which makes category mistakes) since at least the 1920s in the United States that we can move on without much more citation.

Less familiar is the choice to make category mistakes about science and to shrug off all Hobbesian counsels for scientists to be humble that has emerged early in this new millennium. Some of the voguish "new atheism" is advanced by scientists who bring good credentials to their sciences; yet, at the same time, they play into the hands of the creationists — or feed off them — when they use scientific means to "disprove the existence of God" as their main tool to abolish religion. Some of them undertake acts of destruction with polemical charges and bizarre counsel, such as when they urge the world to abolish religion. Then, they urge, utopias of rationalism can emerge without being threatened by the religious barbarians.

We may look at a prominent if not fundamental issue for them: proving or disproving the existence of God. While some contemporary theologians and philosophers do address the issues code-named "the existence of God" through reason, they are speaking to fellow specialists. What they do can be appropriate and creative, but they are seldom affecting those religionists who make up their minds and then base their commitments on grounds not reached by this debate. Such believers may be mindful of what scientists discover and propose as science; they may even be capable of being scientists themselves — indeed, some of them are. And they are clearly rational beings. But they do not wait for philosophers to prove the existence of God in the normal way people speak of "proving." How would they as believers "know" if they had proved, or the atheists had disproved, the existence of God? The enlightened millions among them through the ages made up their minds about ultimate reality independently of scholarly or laboratory proofs. Their descendants are put off by the noisy claims that argument is the only way to bring "distinctive voices" to the exchanges.

While reading the philosopher Oakeshott over a couple of decades, I was learning about conversation from conversations I was having with the theologian David Tracy. I can testify that some learning-through-conversation goes on not via written texts or face-to-face conversation. For three decades, my study at the university adjoined Tracy's, and I often said that much of my theology during that period came from vibrations that my wall picked up and advanced, or by osmosis, or capillary action. This physical transmission was reinforced by the classes that we co-taught, our endless dialogues, and my overhearing of his dealing with students, colleagues, and visitors. This formidable and formative Catholic theologian struck me as being unmatched as a pursuer of the "arrests of experience" that are appropriate for a theologian. Yet he sustained mutually rewarding dialogue with scientists, historians, poets, teachers of myth, and more. In one course we dealt with the issue of pluralism in complex cultures, and Tracy wrote at book length about the issue. In it he focused, as Oakeshott had, on the way one can grow into humility enough to learn and keep contributing to "the human condition." He theorized about conversation just as he practiced it.

Conversation, in Tracy's life and book, "is not a confrontation. It is not a debate. It is not an exam. It is questioning itself. It is a willingness to follow the question wherever it may go. It is dia-logue." Tracy's observations are very direct:

> Conversation is a game with some hard rules: say only what you mean; say it as accurately as you can; listen to and respect what the other says, however different or other; be willing to correct or defend your opinions if challenged by the conversation partner; be willing to argue if necessary, to confront if demanded, to endure necessary conflict, to change your mind if the evidence suggests it. These are merely some generic rules for questioning. As good rules, they are worth keeping in mind in case the questioning does begin to break down. In a sense they are merely variations of the transcendental imperatives elegantly articulated by Bernard Lonergan. "Be attentive, be intelligent, be responsible, be loving, and, if necessary, change."[4]

Some may think that I am investing too much hope in the promise of conversation as a bid for trust, in this case among the distinctive voices of scientists, religionists, and responsible figures in public and political life. It certainly is not a whole program, and one may even say that it is given boundaries by the concerns of Hobbes to promote humility as well as the ability to be attentive, responsible, and changeable when other distinctive voices are heard. It does not mean that trust is-

4. David Tracy, *Plurality and Ambiguity* (San Francisco: Harper and Row, 1987), pp. 18-19.

sues are all resolved through its use. Far from it. Conversation does not suffice when difficulties within one specialty or another demand address. Yet conversation promotes understandings of various kinds, approaches that encourage trust, when the invitation to converse has been extended. A person faces the other and makes tentative intellectual moves, and by that turning she has "disarmed" herself, become vulnerable and searching, and thus potentially trustworthy. This approach is not designed to be helpful in all instances where distrust has to be replaced by trust; but it does directly address the area I have chosen to perceive as holding neglected promise in a time of crisis between and among scientists, religionists, and agents of change in public life.

My choice to begin by imagining and typifying four individuals might have led to the notion that the conversations we are to envision are always intimate, face-to-face, and isolated. However, my intention is to extrapolate on the basis of this picture to groups, collectives, large components of culture. By no means do all scientists agree with each other, and it is confusing and almost unfair to speak of "science" versus "religion" as if one could do justice to reality by such gross lumping and generalizing. In fact, to enter the disciplinary fields of science is to become part of the company of those who are called to differ, to argue, and to test. Nor do all priests agree with each other and think alike. There are 38,000 different denominations in the Christian world, and hundreds of thousands of individuals make up the cohort of pastors, priests, and professors in each. To become ordained or commissioned in one or another of those religious groups is to be committed to the faithful observances of that faith. The same goes for historians and poets, the artists and writers and composers who exercise their imaginations no matter what "the facts" may be.

After I have said that, however, it remains true that those who do not make category mistakes are those who recognize that they are viewing the world and inheriting or forming a discourse in a particular way. They betray their cause and confuse their publics if they do not reflect their modes of experience or give distinctive voice in their speaking. Students of the art of conversation describe motives for engaging in it, offering whole lists of purposes. Conversation furthers education, helps entertain, builds social circles, and is a scene where participants can seek to build trust. Public life provides an arena and a test of conversations that are devoted to the building of cultures of trust.

CHAPTER 7

Where Science and Religion Meet: Public Life

M any intellectual endeavors and exercises meet in public life. While we have concentrated on the worlds of science and religion, the people who occupy them and the institutions that support or express them in public, one could as well include the worlds of health care, education, commerce, and others to illustrate the possibilities. Having set out to make the case that clashes, conflicts, and mutual misunderstandings among scientists and religionists are among the most common and fateful sorts, I will return to them as a case study. Let the religious person pray in private and the scientist work alone in the laboratory; yet, sooner or later, they and other specialists experiment with "going public." Or, pushed by their work and the demands of others, they enter the public realm. The consequences of their efforts may show up tardily, and their effects look like compromises in the public realm but, it is proper to say, "You never know when. . . ."

The Private "Goes Public" and Turns Controversial

Of course, the public can ignore personal enterprises and private strivings, and most of these will remain obscure. Still, who could foresee when St. Francis or Martin Luther might rise from prayer, even in a cloister, to upset the world? Could it have been foreseen that the Karl Marx who scribbled in a dark corner of the British Museum would later publish work that changed the lives of hundreds of millions into a third century? What happens when the William James who quietly studied how the mind works and what happens to speech rose and changed the lives of many who will never hear of him? Figures such as these influence others who make up the larger populace. Where significant leaders who are prominent in the scientific and religious cultures are creative, public consequences follow. Where more positive relationships of trust develop among them, improvement in understanding between the two can occur. Nor is the cost of mistrust or the promise of trust among scientists and religious people confined to the personal lives of leaders, since these leaders engage in work that has effects on huge constituencies and, in some respects, whole populations.

Negative consequences of self-segregated or battling scientists and religionists form the headline-grabbing version of their relationships. For instance, for a century and a half, conflicts over religious and scientific teaching about the origin of the universe have upset the public and required address. Copernicus and Galileo, who had helped evoke the issues, are simply the most invoked symbols of the conflict of science with and within the church. Centuries later — into our time in the United States — so powerful are the voices and so strong the political influences of one particular religious front, self-labeled "scientific creationism," that destructive stalemates have developed. Some legislators have set up barriers against teaching evolution, and some scientists have been distracted from endeavors that could have benefited others. Surveys show that in many locales the majority of the American people, given a stark choice between the mislabeled alternatives "evolution" and "creation," choose to support "creation" on religious and even specifically biblical lines — as they interpret the texts. Some members of the elites in education and jurisprudence quickly get drawn in to what soon become legal and very public matters.

Where "evolutionist" and "anti-evolutionist" forces engage each other, arguments immediately turn political, which means that they deal more with power than with inquiry and experiment. Most scientists who are acquainted with the field of controversy say that eliminating or opposing the teaching of evolution in high schools and colleges is a factor in producing a scientifically illiterate generation. So many aspects of microbiology and other scientific specialties are based on evolutionary thought and understanding that progress in science, whether in the laboratory or as a collection of instruments in culture, is jeopardized.

Meanwhile, from the other side, many conservative religious parents and leaders become so polemically poised against evolutionary theories and related scientific pursuits that they discourage young people from studying science because they deem it harmful to faith. The talent pool of American students of science declines. The universities and laboratories have to depend on imported — most notably Asian — talent. Scientific research depends on vast expenditures of funds, many of them governmental, as in the case of National Institute of Health subsidies, which get reduced when some members of the public rebel.

The cost to society is obviously high whenever there are fights over evolution and many other kinds of scientific teaching in public institutions, or when those fights have their effects in medical procedures and care. Scientists, most of whom are ill equipped by their training to argue philosophy or ethics, are often required to defend themselves or waste time making their case before legislative and funding agencies. To observe this stir is not to say that scientists should go unchallenged, or that they are by any means always correct in the positions they hold or the ventures they propose. Suspicion or criticism, properly aimed and pursued, is something scientists should welcome, because being mindful of it and addressing it can lead scientists to do what their vocation and profession demand: to question basic assumptions and monitor scientific experiments and claims. Science demands questioning, not always only by scientists: those in the humanities and social sciences, religious thinkers among them, are often well motivated and equipped to help improve the sciences by the questions they ask when they are not being sent out on trivial and destructive missions.

To put it bluntly and basically: religionists can "know" things that scientists as scientists do not necessarily "know" if they follow their charters or work on their agendas. If the quality of the critiques and questioning improve, science improves; and when science improves, potentials in human life grow. My university, the University of Chicago, from its nineteenth-century beginnings, has had as its motto *Crescat Scientia — Vita Excolatur.* No one is quite sure of the origin of that saying, and there has been considerable confusion leading to argument among those who try to explore it. In paraphrase, some founder insisted and proclaimed that where science grows and prospers, there human life is enhanced. "Science" here does not mean science in the curricular confines of divisions or departments of science; it means "knowing" in the larger sense. Nor would defenders of the motto have a good case claiming that most science will enrich life all the time. Some research can produce poison gases or promote genetic tampering of a dangerous kind. Still, whatever the risks in and the price paid to the sciences, thoughtful people know that wholesale rejection or paralyzing suspicion of it will hurt medical research, for example, and lead to more illness and the failure to find life-giving cures.

While it may be less fashionable in some circles to say so, and may even be puzzling to those who have not analyzed them, religious cultures ordinarily are also committed to "knowing" and to "learning." When religious thinkers restrain themselves and avoid category mistakes that lead to irrelevant or passionate political conflicts, they also demonstrate the potential of enhancing life. They ask their own kinds of questions as they rely on appropriate "modes of experience" and "voices of distinction." They can provide inspiration as well as silence, and they can motivate young people to explore more dimensions of life, including lives in science, and pursue professions, vocations, and careers. To quote Pascal is to risk introducing apparent ignorance into scenes of complexity. But Pascal was right to notice that the heart *does* have its reasons that reason does not know. Ask lovers, new parents, or those who care for relatives who are ill or in need, and it will become obvious that an obsession with a rationalism that excludes a variety of human meanings will miss learning much that is worth knowing — even vital — about human existence. The wrong kinds of questions and criticism may cause many to stop at the brink of unconventional research in areas where science and faith overlap. Examples of this appear in inquiries into what faith can provide with respect to physical healing.

Open conversations among scientists and religionists can be creative because they do not have to "settle" anything. Nowadays we hear of physicists and cosmologists who are working on a "theory of everything," which is designed to answer questions about why there is a universe and how it works. One reads the page-long collections of numbers and symbols proposed by those who claim to be closing in on such an encompassing theory. Suppose that some year soon such physicists come up with Absolute Proof that they have been successful. Their claims will put them on page one and give them prime-time media coverage — and deservedly so. Those symbols will represent a great achievement. Yet it is not difficult to imagine that soon opposing schools of thought — on the model of "big bang" theory versus "anti-big bang" theory or "string" theory versus "anti-string" theory — will stake their claims. It is not likely, however, that if the proponents of such theories advance or support them, there will be fewer religionists a day after the announcement. Reverse all this and it will be apparent that no envisionable religious claim to have found the Absolute Truth for All would stand up to scrutiny and hold the field. Levels of mistrust among and between scientists and religionists would likely increase.

To picture this is not to romanticize conversation or to detract from the potential of argument. Conversing is a limited art, and it defers to argument in many cases. When it is time to come to conclusions or make proposals, argument — one hopes of a creative kind — has to be the chosen instrument. This will be evident in debates within public schools or when legislators and educators have to establish budgets and determine priorities. Argument is necessary and can be creative if there is to be any measure of justice in a republic, because conflicts of interest have to be arbitrated and the varieties of interests in some measure have to be satisfied. Budgets and apportionments for scientific ventures that have political implications — government-supported stem-cell research being at issue most recently — involve interest groups and demand argument. As with conversation, so with argument at its best: creative outcomes rely on the ability of contending parties to be trustworthy and to act with trust. Human weakness and failure being what they are, misrepresentation, deceit, and overt lying compose a shadow over many incidents where negotiation and contention are at work. However, the healthier the cultures of trust become, the better it is for argument.

The Public and the Political

German philosopher Jürgen Habermas introduced and developed the language of "the public sphere" in efforts to imagine or prescribe a zone where the various interests and voices get represented. While his proposal has met with many kinds of criticism, these do not affect what is at issue here, namely, that promoting trust among those who come with diverse "modes of experiences" or "voices" governing their positions have to at least begin meeting and understanding.[1] Such a sphere

---

1. Jürgen Habermas, *The Structural Transformation of the Public Sphere: An Inquiry into a Category of Bourgeois Society* (Cambridge, MA: MIT Press, 1989).

is located, as are subcultures in our contexts, between the private sphere and the public spheres of authority, such as the state. The public sphere is the scene of discourse, often of a sort that has an impact on both the private sphere and public authority. Whether in Habermas's or anyone else's terms, the move from purely individual perceptions, or the "subcultures" of trust, eventually impels the public into quasi-political arenas. There trust is most difficult to achieve, and there it is most necessary. In short, sooner or later within a republic a "culture of trust" must represent as much of the public as possible. Anarchists and authoritarians rule themselves out on this point, though they also have to be taken into account by those who would envision and promote a larger and more inclusive culture of trust.

At this transition it is also important to make a distinction between *public,* which is the genus, and *politics,* which is the species. Much of my own career has been devoted to the subject of "religion and public life," and the name of a center, a lectureship, and a professorship associate me with "public religion," "public theology," or "the public church." In all cases, those who do the naming and the assigning of missions and all those who work to advance them have to make clear that they do not want "public" to be reduced to "politics," as vital and protean as the reach of politics may be. Conversation about cultures of trust certainly has to begin somewhere other than in politics, which is both a test and one of the hardest zones in which to achieve growth in trust.

Conversation about a public cannot easily move from the experience of a public order in which trust is lacking to one in which some measures of trust are evident. For success in building cultures of trust, there has to be a long-term cultivation of trust in numerous spheres and zones. Publics have to find motivation to improve the politics of trust. They will lack motivation, of course, if they do not know anything about each other, or when they cannot understand where the other "is coming from." Worst is when the other is described to them by those who have strong motivations to create suspicion or destroy the potential for trust in others. Through self-reflection, conversation, many kinds of cultural interaction, and, yes, argument, elements of the public learn the face of the other or can interpret the voice of the other. They can avoid category mistakes and similar irrelevancies, discern what gestures and practices mean, and find out what leads to defensiveness in the self and in the other. Then politics can be contentious but positive, not merely destructive.

Parker Palmer has described the "public" in these broader terms.[2] To paraphrase his proposals: the public refers to all the places where the subcommunities, groups, and interests come to share the same place, be it a forum, a mall, a college, a town meeting. It may make its appearance in the theater and the concert hall, the precinct headquarters and the meeting places of interest groups, alumni associations, and perhaps even via the flawed instrument of opinion surveys. There the color and texture of the "company of strangers" are on public display, and people make charges and set up defenses — and sometimes even develop friendships. In the public zones there can be tests of the scope of both conflict and consensus. In a sense, the public sphere can be a place for testing the waters of politics and providing contexts for political activities. An example: a city threatened by political conflict on racial issues comes together at professional athletic events or concerts featuring blues, spirituals, jazz, and classical music in public parks. They allow for serendipitous contacts, friendly encounters, and a community spirit that can transcend or outlast political conflict.

We appear to have moved from our starting point, where the cultures of trust begin in the experience of the individual, the smallest "unit" for the theorizing and practice of trust. "I trust you." "Do you trust me?" "Have I given you a reason to trust me?" "How do we leave behind distrust, having learned from the experiences of unsettlement?" In the intimate and less-than-public zone, betrayal hurts the most, though it will obviously cause fewer negative public effects than in some larger spheres. Yet they interact and interpenetrate each other. Thus honesty made evident in a neighborhood or a small-town store is more immediately experienced, or its absence more desperately felt, than where trust is broken in the large megalopolitan complex, the vast cluster city and its satellites. In those settings, face-to-face interaction is rare and sometimes virtually disappears. Yet the bid for trust only grows more intense, and the stakes are raised in that impersonal world, including the political sphere, which is such a focal part of the public.

2. Parker Palmer, *The Company of Strangers: Christians and the Renewal of America's Public Life* (New York: Crossroad, 1983).

Trust within Public Institutions and Expressions, Ending with Politics

A quick sweep of the public sphere reveals a considerable number of institutions and expressions, each of which demands and has elicited much scrutiny. Each of them can represent segments or layers in the figurative building of trust. Begin with the media, on which so much spreading of suspicion and distrust depends. The media play roles in the public sphere so evident that they need no documentation. The character of competitive advertising claims on radio and television and the many preachments of broadcasters and writers who bid for listeners, viewers, and readers to accept with little question what they have to offer greatly enlarges the sphere where mistrust grows. Similarly, the economy — here I mean the worlds of business, commerce, and investment — depends on varieties of trust, often reinforced by guarantees in contracts and pledges (or so the public hopes). The economy engenders a host of reasons for requiring trust and yet expressing distrust. Third, education on all levels represents efforts to show that there can be trust — but also the appearances of failed trust. Further, voluntary associations such as charitable organizations, religious institutions, and many more are naturally made up of diverse people. They bring in differing interests, and they show a desire for *some* kind of sustained trust. It almost goes without saying that the public sphere, which also includes all dimensions of health care and relief, demands trust. This is true because citizens must take a high risk on account of their remoteness from those who would like to check up on them, control them, or exact something from them.

Politics and Trust, Democracy and Trust

Finally — and mentioning it here is not surprising — there is politics, involving explicit political action. An important recent book-length approach to the subject is Mark E. Warren's *Democracy and Trust*.[3] A professor at Georgetown University, Warren brought together ten contributors from American universities, people who do not always agree with

3. Mark E. Warren, ed., *Democracy and Trust* (Cambridge: Cambridge University Press, 1999), p. 1.

each other but all of whom represent important voices on the subject. If "politics" is a species of the genus "public," then "democracy," with its need for citizen trust, focuses the question even more. Warren opens the symposium with an attempt to show what he observes and means in the political order before he elaborates in two other relevant paragraphs. First the definition: "Trust involves a judgment, however implicit, to accept vulnerability to the potential ill will of others by granting them discretionary power over some good. When one trusts, one accepts some amount of risk for potential harm in exchange for the benefits of cooperation."[4]

Warren is here picking up on the most consistent factor in the issuance of trust toward one another or toward an institution: the subject of risk, to which I have pointed so frequently. If there is no risk, there is no need for trust. If there is too much risk, extending any trust is folly. If gauging a situation for its risk and trust is complex in one-on-one relations, it is even more so when one deals with collectives, as with parties, candidates, and nations. In this complicated situation, there has to be some balancing or compensating factor, which Warren, relying on economic transactions, uses for analogies. For instance, when I enter into political trust situations, I have to have confidence that I will receive benefits. By referring to these, nothing so flagrant as a bribe or payoff has to be involved. Instead, the benefits are those that come with the proceeds of democratic existence, including freedom, agency, and potential productivity. Since "I" want these and "you" collectively can perhaps help deliver them, I can take the risk. A culture of trust allows for such measurements of risks and benefits.

Another factor tucked into that picturing of trust situations is another exchange: I give "you" (the individual or collective other) the potential for "some good," but you (this "other") must use your discretionary power. To gain in a transaction, I give up something, which here means I surrender something of my invulnerability. To make this point, Warren cites Annette Baier, one of the most trusted writers on trust: "Where one depends on another's good will, one is necessarily vulnerable to the limits of that good will. One leaves others an opportunity to harm one when one trusts, and also shows one's confidence that they will not take it."[5] Warren concludes: "So if I extend trust I am also judg-

4. See also Annette Baier, "Trust and Antitrust," *Ethics* 96: 231-60.
5. Baier, "Trust and Antitrust," p. 235.

ing — however habitually or tacitly — that my trust will not be abused." The assumption behind all this political trusting is that "there is no essential conflict of interest between myself and the person to whom I extend trust, or at least no conflict of interest that is not mitigated by other relationships, securities, or protections."[6]

What sounds cozy and intimate on the personal level, where the stakes that go with trust can already be high, is rendered more complex still by the fact that "the assumption of solidarity with others often is suspect, and herein lies the ambiguous, even paradoxical, nature of the topic of democracy and trust." One can see these investments and calculations, Warren notes, in the flux of partisan politics and shifting allegiances during primary election contests. This is followed by awareness of the need to refashion solidarity with fellow party members whom one may have opposed minutes before the final votes were counted — all with an eye on the new partisan electoral foe.

All this cannot be based on anything so unstable as emotion, though emotional or affective life can help "seal the deal" when one extends and receives trust. In the end — and one does not have to be a rationalist to perceive this — the trusting act is heavily cognitive, based on thought-out and rehearsed calculations. Warren calls this the "cognitive dimension," and with that in mind he quotes Russell Hardin: "Trust is in a cognitive category with knowledge. To say 'I trust you' means that I know or think I know relevant things about you, especially about your motivations toward me. It is such knowledge that many of us cannot sensibly claim to have with respect to most government officials or with respect to government generally [or, I would add, to public life, politics in general]."[7] Similarly, one could make the case for trust that is developed on affective, emotional, moral, or aesthetic grounds. In the latter case, devotees of classical music are drawn to events, personalities, and experiences through which they bond with others, and in the light of which they compare notes and refine positions, thus building trust. On the other hand, aficionados of jazz music similarly build trust among each other, but we do not expect the separate "tastes" of the two cohorts to lead to easy transmission of reasons for trust.

6. Warren, *Democracy and Trust,* p. 1.

7. Russell Hardin, "Do We Want Trust in Government?" in Warren, *Democracy and Trust,* p. 24.

Trust, Interest, and Self-interest

To deal with the complications of trust on the democratic-political scene, Russell Hardin develops a novel concept that he calls "encapsulated interest." It translates as follows: "To say that I trust you with respect to some matter means that I have reason to expect *you to act in my interest* with respect to that matter because you have good reasons to do so, *reasons that are grounded in my interest.* In other words, to say that I trust you means I have reason to expect you to act, for your own reasons, *as my agent* with respect to the relevant matter. Your interest encapsulates my interest."[8] This concept recognizes the limits of human generosity and risk, and it relies on some measure of self-interest on the part of both and all parties.

Warren is clear about the assumptions concerning human nature and experience. One may believe in self-interest based on inheritance from simian ancestry, Augustine's "original sin," or Karl Rahner's what "ought not to be," which means, in other words, to have a "low" expectation of the other in whom one is to trust — and in oneself, the truster — and still find reason to take the risks. Here are some options in any realm of human life, whether it has to do with a person's committing to play in an orchestra, serve on a hospital board, follow a candidate, or vote. One must act, but how must one do so?

First, one can ignore the issue of trust except when a crisis comes. Thus a young man may not give much thought to the question of loyalty to country until war breaks out, whereupon he is drafted and placed under command in life-and-death situations. He is there assessing risks in a rather closed situation. He is loyal and has to trust, or else he will be subject, for example, to court martial. "Ignoring" is not a good strategy if one wants a healthy public life as a citizen.

It is possible to be as blithe as an unthinking fellow citizen if one chooses to greet occasions in public life in a spirit of open optimism. Eric M. Uslander, in an essay in the Warren anthology, speaks of this: "Optimists believe that other people will be helpful . . . ; they have faith in their own capacity to shape the world. Optimists are not worried that others will exploit them. If they take a chance and lose, their upbeat world view leads them to try again. . . . So it makes sense to trust others." Optimism can produce some good effects, since it "leads to generalized

---

8. Hardin, "Do We Want Trust?" p. 26 (emphasis in original).

trust, which promotes civic activism, which creates a prosperous community, leading to increasing optimism. Pessimistic people trust only their own kind."[9] But what about those who are neither optimists or pessimists — on ontological or experiential grounds? Some who fill the portrait of Plato's Glaucon or Hobbes's natural man can be pessimists, but the cognitive dimension of trusting has to come in somewhere along the way to offer responsible alternatives. Hope for positive effects in the long pull of democracy's contests and possibilities can lead some to enjoy the luxury of optimistic moments and outlooks. However, the human record suggests that something more than optimism — or pessimism, we hasten to add — has to color the search for the trustworthy in public life.

Thus, to give the appearance of reinforcing the structures of trust and to develop some kind of culture of public trust, publics regularly resort to some policies of coercion. Anything but a utopian philosophy forces citizens to back up their cognitive and emotional investments in trust with resort to protection. This may take the form of gated communities, providing insurance, and supporting effective law enforcement. All of these are legitimate, sometimes necessary, but necessarily not sufficient means. Citizens can in many ways seek to eliminate risk, but public life would have to assume a reliance on force of almost unimaginable weight. The more advisable choice for citizens at that point, however, would be to assess their own "encapsulated" interests on which they can trade when they would deal with the other. An illustration via a poem by Ralph Waldo Emerson can point to personal dimensions of this commitment to self and other.

The Props That Surround Trust

Citing this poem by Emerson may seem to be nothing more than a relief from a demanding part of the discussion of politics and trust, or "political trust." People associate Emerson with poetic softness, vagueness, or what one cruel critic called his *Incomprehensibilityositivityalityation-mentnessism*. Politics, meanwhile, is conventionally associated with prosaic hardness and clarity. How can the two mix or reinforce each other?

9. Eric M. Uslander, "Democracy and Social Capital," in Warren, *Democracy and Trust*, pp. 138-40.

Emerson's short poem, not about trust but about grace, illustrates some ways. We will take a close look at the poem and then connect it analogously to trust and my approach to the subject.

Grace

How much, Preventing God, how much I owe
To the defenses thou hast round me set;
Example, custom, fear, occasion slow, —
These scorned bondmen were my parapet.
I dare not peep over this parapet
To gauge with glance the roaring gulf below,
The depths of sin to which I had descended,
Had not these me against myself defended.

Casual readers and many critics have been puzzled as to how Emerson, the author of "Self-Reliance," could put so much faith in nothing but relationships with others and put so little trust in his own inner resources.

The first clue we get to what is going on is that Emerson has a new prefix or attribute for God. Instead of "provident" or "providing" God, he has "Preventing God." If God was provident and providing in ordinary theistic belief in Emerson's day, in this poem God takes on a very specific role: it is God's task, manner, or call to "prevent" bad things from happening. Readers can see why this preventing is a key to our approach to building cultures of trust. Had the bad things happened, the poet knew he would have descended into depths of sin, which for us would mean he would have occasioned distrust or acted on the basis of trust denied or betrayed. "Preventing God" is invoked more personally than in most of Emerson's work, and the action of this God is precise: to set up defenses.

A second key element in the Emersonian approach to grace — and here by analogy to trust — is his assessment of himself as an agent in transacting trust. Remarkably, therefore, the enemy in question in the poem is "myself," the self that would have otherwise descended into "sin," which is also not a word we would usually expect to see coming out of Emerson's rhetorical bag. Emerson pictures his own self as surrounded by defenses, since he would have succumbed or plunged had he not this circling set of defenses. Ordinarily, he would have scorned such defenses, and would have still spoken negatively as he compared them to "scorned bondmen." Apart from them, he was usually in the company of the scornful. Not now.

Has he known experiences of a positive kind that his contemporaries who were evangelicals valued, and have they assigned these to grace? Hardly. In their eyes, his use of the term "grace" here sounds ironic and may seem to be a categorical mistake. He is not "freed" — as they would say *they* were — by grace. Instead, he is set into bondage by four scorned bondmen. Yet he sounds like traditional givers of praise do, since he addresses God — very uncharacteristically — as personal, and he acknowledges the role of the typical debtor, who offers virtual thanks.

The four bondmen are all key to developing the political culture of trust. First, take the bondman *example.* Where political trust was absent or had almost wholly broken down, the poet or anyone for whom he speaks would have fallen into an abyss of despair. Absent political trust, governments and citizens would seem to have two choices: they can turn totalitarian and subject the citizen to nothing but un-graced, coercive life, far from any democratic ideals; or they can let go of the bonds and permit anarchy and chaos to displace "-archy" and order, which would result in Hobbesian existence at its worst, and the jungle would prevail.

For Emerson, though, there is one alternative that appears to be less dramatic than the other two: *example.* While some readings of history suggest that not a single individual in a polity and certainly in a government rises above the alternatives of enslavement or anarchy, even in the worst circumstances some individuals do keep trust and elicit trust from subjects or fellow citizens. If examination of a particular breakdown offers no example, then a person can look next door, anywhere else, into myth, Scripture, or historical records of heroism.

"Example" here can be related to the word *exemplum* in medieval Latin lexicons. As John D. Lyon has pointed out, if we picture such tomes as anticipations of the Oxford English Dictionary — which means "on historical principles" and with the offering of samples of usage — the medieval wordsmith would say that, for *exemplum,* one is to think of something cut out, selected, or, in a metaphorical sense, to imagine a clearing in the woods.[10] One pictures the clearing in the

---

10. John D. Lyon, *Exemplum: The Rhetoric of Example in Early Modern France and Italy* (Princeton, NJ: Princeton University Press, 1989).

woods as a place where definition occurs: there the woods stop and the line of clearing begins. A positive example in politics is the individual, party, or movement that defines where untrustworthiness ends and where, in all its complexity, trustworthiness begins.

To the lexicographer who alludes to "a clearing in the woods" as another expression of exemplarity, the clearing is where the light falls. The woods are thick and dark as Dante saw them when, at the beginning of his poem, he spoke of finding himself in the middle of his life in a dark wood. Thus one can see that the exemplar typically sheds light to pursue other ways. When there are reasons for distrust in politics, reformers shed the light of publicity that exposes underground or underhanded moves that work ill on the body politic. If Emerson ordinarily looked out on the American scene in the nineteenth century with the skeptical eye that he brought to most of the politics he viewed, here he could turn to "example," the people he honored, as in the American Constitutional period, who had spread light and were the enemy of anyone who countered or weakened trust.

Third, in the instance of the lexicographer who adduced "clearing in the woods," the *exemplum* could be a place for cultivation. Under the canopy of trees and on the forest floor many kinds of growth could and did occur. But they offered only some of the goods and foods a society needs. There had to be cleared places where farmers could cultivate, teachers could teach "kindergarten," and delicate growth of what might become full-blown trust-relations could be developed.

Building political cultures of trust also depends on tradition, or *custom.* Political scientists can even speak of "change" or "revolution," but they still have to draw on what has gone before. So the second of Emerson's "scorned bondmen" who guarded his self as if on a walled parapet was "custom." When mistrust or untrustworthiness characterizes life in a polity, citizens can draw not only on example but on custom. Of course, any prop one could offer for proper formation, reform, or new endeavors will be ambiguous, as is most of what matters in complex human affairs. This is especially true in politics, where diverse wills and ideas are in conflict. So custom can be impoverishing and enslaving. It is "customary" in some governments to take bribes, tell lies, undercut opponents, engage in graft, and deliberately mislead in public relations. At the same time, many people who have values and integrity bring them to office and often have helped set up patterns of government in which good customs are allowed to develop.

Custom and Cultures of Trust

The positive side of custom is also available and necessary when developing cultures of trust. When one hears "that simply isn't done around here," the person who says it is not invoking law, whether written or oral. She is not saying, "It's up to you whether you want to bribe, lie, slander, or graft." She is saying or implying, "The people who lead and work here have worked consistently on policies and practices that breed trust. We are counting on you to contribute to that practice and image." Júlian Marías and José Ortega y Gasset drew on a Spanish term to describe this: *vigencias.* The translator of Marías's *Generations: A Historical Method* has provided a helpful footnote, one that suggests immediately how appropriate it is in this Emersonian context:

> *Vigencia* is related to that which has life *(quod viget).* They are social forces arising from many sectors of life and imposed on us without the intervention of our will. They are binding, impersonal forces that form the very fabric of the collectivity.

And in the text itself, Marías writes:

> *Vigencias,* or binding customs . . . [are] social usages, beliefs, and current ideas which are imposed on individuals automatically. Individuals find themselves living in the midst of usages with their impersonal and anonymous pressure. This does not mean that the individual must necessarily yield to the demands of current customs, but he does have to be aware of them; he must confront them in order to accept or reject them.[11]

Note that the word "binding" appears in the text and the footnote alike. Here, binding customs can enhance the quest to display trust if the customs lead those who inherit them to be aware of the ways in which some of them can further develop this quest.

Both political leaders and voters who are subjects may increase mistrust by following the wrong kind of binding customs. In Italy, for example, news accounts report that millions cheat openly on income

---

11. Júlian Marías, *Generations: A Historical Method,* trans. Harold C. Raley (Tuscaloosa: University of Alabama Press, 1967), p. 81.

taxes and do not pay them. In such a culture, those citizens who do in-herit and inhabit worlds where the customs are positive can begin to win back approaches that will improve civil life.

The third Emersonian defense can easily be translated into an ex-perience of searching and building that can be positive. Emerson did not trust "grace" to keep himself from having to "gauge . . . the depths of sin to which [he] had descended. . . ." Plato's Glaucon instantly comes to mind again as the agent of fear-mongering who illustrated the base for all the trust that matters. This means the presence of the fear of get-ting caught in an era in which electronic surveillance is becoming so constant and far-reaching. One might be exposed when breaking trust. Or it can be a fear of the chaos that might ensue even if the perpetrator of mistrust is not caught by the surveillance camera or apprehended by detectives. We need not say much about that at this point, since fear is somehow or other at the base of penal codes, practices, and policing threats. A person fears lest being caught in a lie or a breach of trust will cause him to be brought to court. Another fears opinion — of family and society — and so acts in a way that leads to a different course and one that exemplifies trust to the point that her actions respond to "binding customs" and follow the examples of others.

In the poem "Grace," Emerson adds one more defensive agent to keep himself from sinning, as one does when one corrupts efforts to keep trust, and he calls it *"occasion slow."* I am neither a sufficient po-etry critic nor Emerson scholar to speak with authority on what the two-word phrase means, but "example," "custom," and "fear" should by themselves have become so familiar and intelligible that we do not need his fourth protection, and we can let it go at that. Suffice it to say that we should have clues to move, as Emerson did, beyond self-centered concern and overcommitment to a possibly wrong social con-nection. Neither the totalitarians nor the anarchists should hold the field. There are ways to build measures of trust, which I have been call-ing meliorative and incremental as I outline them in this chapter.

Trust in the Constant Context of Risk

Claus Offe, yet another contributor to the Warren symposium, has ad-dressed the persistent issue of risk. He helpfully applies general talk about trust to politics in the most explicit senses. I share his understanding of what he calls a "three-step argument."[12] First, three major media of coordination complicate and force the issue of trust, and they are evident in all concerted political activity. They are money, authority, and knowledge.

Offe concentrates on four levels as he approaches these. The first we have been addressing, which is the at least minimal reflexive trust citizens ordinarily have for each other or "everyone else." This is the one-on-one or intimate level of trust. Second, we pay attention in public life to "mass constituencies" in political elites and in other sectors. Among these, Offe mentions "the churches, the media, the police, the court system, the military, or the medical professions," all of which provide key opportunities for developing cultural modes of trust.

For such cultures to progress and build trust on broader levels, a third level of interaction is crucial, as I have pointed out when discussing scientific and religious elites and participants. Offe calls this "the horizontal trust" extending among political elites as well as others, such as those in business, labor, religions, academia, the military, and so on. One pictures all this as being more difficult to promote than the first two. The fourth depends on the third: "the top-down vertical dimension of trust where elites form beliefs about the behavioral dispositions of sectoral constituencies or entire mass publics." Offe properly argues that what needs most study and attention is the "non-elite" population, where what he calls the level of "horizontal trust" prevails. In short, "How can we trust our fellow citizens?" What conditions have to be met to encourage it? He adds a question that is important in his analysis of markets: "Why is trust at all desirable, beneficial, and arguably, indispensable as a factor of social integration in modern democratic market societies?"

In this elaboration of the topic of risk, Offe confirms what we have read in Warren and others: "Trust is the *belief* concerning the action that is to be expected from others. The belief refers to probabilities that (certain categories of) others will do certain things or refrain from doing certain things, which in either case affects the well-being of the holder of the belief, as well as possibly the well-being of others or a relevant collectivity." As with beliefs in any consideration, there is a chance that they may be wrong. Following beliefs can risk causing damage. The truster

12. Claus Offe, "How Can We Trust Our Fellow Citizens?" in Warren, *Democracy and Trust,* pp. 44-50 (emphasis in original).

knows the risk, but trusts anyhow: "I know it can happen, yet I believe it *won't* happen" — that is, some undesired event that is the fault of the trusted. Remove risk? "One might derive the maxim not to trust anybody before we can be nearly certain about him, at which point, however, much trust is no longer needed." If a person trusts too little and risks nothing, she cuts off many possible and desired outcomes. Over-protectiveness has its price in matters of trusting or not trusting.

Here many factors come into play in all of public life. For instance, time: experience of "the other" who is being monitored usually implies a certain length of observation. Offe reminds us of the obvious: "Trust-building is a very time-consuming activity, while the irreparable destruction of trust can occur in an instant." Hasty judgments are costly when contemplating whether or not to trust. During the experience of assessment, the other who wants to be trusted gives reasons for trusting. By this point, exchange occurs: "Trust obliges the trusted — if only because moral stigma is attached to acts of betraying or exploiting the trust of others." A moral obligation has by this point entered into the reckoning over a trust commitment. People trust, says Offe, both out of considerations of obligation and self-interest, and both demand moral inquiry.

Trust among Strangers

Up to this point we have been discussing situations of trust among those who at least know each other, know something about each other, or share life within institutions, preferably those that are part of cultures of trust. However, trust among strangers is more difficult to experience, and it is precisely such trust that matters most in politics and public life. Quoting S. N. Eisenstadt, Offe again implicitly frames our problem: "The conditions that make for the maintenance of trust are best met in relatively limited ranges of social activities and interaction, such as the family or kinship groups in which social interaction is regulated according to primordial and particularistic criteria."[13] Yet in pub-

---

13. Offe, "How Can We Trust?" pp. 50, 54-55, 57, 70. See S. M. Eisenstadt, *Power, Trust and Meaning: Essays in Sociological Theory and Analysis* (Chicago: University of Chicago Press, 1995), pp. 312-13, 366-67; see also Robert A. Dahl, "The Problem of Civic Competence," *Journal of Democracy* 3 (1992): 53.

lic life one does not have the luxury of relying on the primordial and particular. Students of "civic virtue," such as Robert A. Dahl, pose the issue: If "emphatic understanding, acquired through love, affection, friendship, neighborliness and the like," is the essence of civic virtue, how can it develop in a mass democracy?

Institutions must somehow replace individuals on many levels of trusting in public life. Do I trust this campaign, this party, this fundraising organization? Yet the individuals who make up these institutions still remain important. Offe defends the proposition that leaders matter: "Institutions, well-entrenched and time-honored though they may appear, depend for their viability upon the supportive dispositions and understanding of those involved in them." The substantive quality of institutions, their ability to make sense, determines the degree to which they generate loyalties as a basis for building and keeping trust.

> Institutions, if appropriately designed, can enable us to trust persons whom we have never had contact with and with whom we share no relevant communal allegiance. It is not obvious how this happens, as institutions are not like persons as they cannot themselves be the object of trust. Strictly speaking, only actors can be trusted, as they are the only units capable of reciprocating trust. In contrast, institutions are, first of all, sets of rules. But more than that, they provide normative reference points and values that can be relied upon in order to justify and make sense of those rules. Institutions, in other words, are endowed with a spirit, an ethos, an implicit moral theory, an *idée directrice,* or a notion of some preferred way of conducting the life of the community. My thesis is that *it is this implied normative meaning of institutions and the moral plausibility I assume it will have for others which allows me to trust those that are involved in the same institutions* — although they are strangers and not personally known to me. From "my" point of view, it is the built-in meaning of institutions, its evidence and moral compellingness, that leads "them" to share with "me" a commitment to the norms and values represented by the institutions and thus transforms them, my anonymous fellow citizens, into trustworthy and actually trusted "compatriots."[14]

14. Offe, "How Can We Trust?" p. 70 (emphasis in original).

The Role of Institutions

If we consider institutions to be important bearers of the meanings, symbols, and causes of a culture, it is clear that a culture of trust would depend in no small measure on the quality of its institutions, including, of course, those devoted to science and religion. A whole strategy for developing the cultures can be deduced from Offe's few lines, and he provides four prompts: "Institutions generalize trust to the extent they commit their members to the virtue of *truth-telling*" and monitor and direct them. "I trust anonymous others if I encounter them within a framework of institutionalized honesty and authenticity."

Second, "promise-keeping, and more specifically the virtue of *honoring contracts,* is just the active version of truth-telling." The generalization of trust will proceed best if the values of "fairness, impartiality, and neutrality" are present. And, finally, the leaders of the "institutional regime" relate to and promise to compensate for differences that exist among the strangers that make them up and deal with them.[15]

Institutions are one element in cultures, and cultures provide many opportunities for enhancing trust. The most profound humanistic culture embodies what Ortega describes below:

> It is the conception of the world or the universe which serves as the plan, riskily elaborated by man, for orienting himself among things, for coping with his life, and for finding a direction amid the chaos of his situation. . . . Culture is only the interpretation which man gives to his life, the series of more or less satisfying solutions he finds in order to meet the problems and necessities of life, as well those which belong to the material order as the so-called spiritual ones.[16]

One of Ortega's commentators, Karl Weintraub, adds:

> Every cultural institution, every project of life, every activity, thought, and sentiment is dependent on this core zone of *creencias* from which each culture lives. Political life, economic activity, the sciences

15. Offe, "How Can We Trust?" pp. 73-75.

16. Quoted by Karl J. Weintraub, *Visions of Culture* (Chicago: University of Chicago Press, 1966), pp. 266-67.

and religious beliefs, the arts, the love life of a society, are expressions of this deepest stratum of *trusted* reality.[17]

At the base of political life and trust, I have proposed or at least noted, is argument. At the base of most aspects of public life, necessarily occurring before argument can be fruitful, is conversation. It is all well and good for scientists, religionists, and politicians or public figures to deal with modes of experience, but they must communicate with congenial partners, strangers, and enemies. Key to all the development of cultures of trust is conversation, freshly conceived and explored. So we will converse about conversation.

17. Weintraub, *Visions of Culture*, pp. 266-67 (emphasis added).

CHAPTER 8

How to Build Cultures of Trust Relating Science, Religion, and Public Life

————◦《◦》◦————

B egin a book title with the words "How to . . ." and you invite negative responses from skeptical reviewers who tot up lists from *Books
in Print* and mock the genre. Who is really helped by such writings? Or if
a how-to chapter appears at the end of a book, an author risks jolting
and losing readers who had come along for a scholarly ride, not expecting practical counsel, which often turns out to be too brief and sketchy
to be of much use. One can imagine readers of the preceding seven
chapters agreeing that there is a crisis of trust in the larger society and
culture; however, they may more reluctantly agree that a call to address
the crisis should engage them in some sort of action to follow up on the
exercise in reading and thinking about the issues.

Awareness of such reservations leads me to repeat what I have said
earlier: any constructive addressing of this subject has to be modest
and can only take the form of tentative suggestions for change. The
scholarly voice within me also says that contributions of an intellectual
kind, writings that promote understanding, have or should have intrinsic value and need not be practical. Readers of works on ancient Egyp-
tian dynasties, or tadpoles, or Persian rugs, or the poetry of Wallace
Stevens are not called to rise from a library chair and then book passage
to Cairo, gaze into pools of water, buy a loom, or start writing poems.
Similarly, the reader of a treatise on the breakdown of trust among, for
example, scientists and religionists does not need to become a partisan
at debates or a drafter of new programs in order to have profited from
the reading.

Still, calling attention to the proposition that between the extreme poles of utopian folly or cultural despair there is value in building cultures and subcultures of trust is an implicit call to point to alternatives to such extremes. The concept of "building cultures" shows up rather infrequently in the literature. I have located a few instances in which writers do speak of building, for example, cultures of teaching, innovation, or shared leadership. The most formal use of the concept appears in a goal of the United Religions Institute (URI), which would teach people "how to build cultures of peace, justice, and healing" — both globally and locally. I note that in recent literature the URI speaks not of "building" but of "creating" such cultures; but we will stay with the metaphor of constructing such cultures and subcultures — with good reason.

Universes of Discourse, Though Distinct, Are Not Isolated

Efforts to contribute to cultures of trust can easily be frustrated if the distinct *modes of experience* or the *universes of discourse* that are characteristic of the spheres of science, religion, and, to some extent, politics as an expression within public life — the three spheres that have made up our case study — would make it impossible to communicate. Failure to understand these modes, or to misapply them, easily leads to category mistakes, "the most fatal of all errors," since they signal irrelevance across the boundaries of the worlds or spheres. Because each of these modes or universes represents in many ways incompatible voices, culture could be seen as cut up into sealed compartments. Voices then would take the form of muffled soliloquies and would never enjoy opportunities for communication or culture-building. Thus, if a scientist cannot understand "where a religionist is coming from," or vice versa, encounters between them could end with nothing accomplished. Trust would not only not be advanced, it would even be diminished.

To suggest moves beyond compartmentalization and cocooned existence, we have paid attention to dialogue of a special kind as the prime means of transcending boundaries and opening the possibility for the "voices in conversation" to promote some common good. Advertising the value of conversation is one thing, but then picturing the voices being in conversation calls for some description of the context in which productive conversation is to go on and does go on. Attention to this envisioning warrants a return to beginnings, by means of recall of the most basic and intimate conversations and experiences of subcultures in which we hear them.

Trust-relations that are closest to home, I have argued, demand and deserve closest attention — for a number of good reasons. First, the word "home" suggests the most personal and immediate zone in which relationships will be found to be positive or negative. Their value will depend on the quality of trust shown among the people under a roof, connected as they may be by ties of blood, or merely living up or down the street in the neighborhood. While most discussions of mistrust or distrust and trust involve trained and professional elites, such as doctors, lawyers, ministers, teachers, or diplomats, every member of the public is engaged in daily negotiations and experiences that concern trust. "We" the public outnumber the members of those elite professions by thousands to one, so we are often affected when trust is broken or when it is kept, when it is fragile or when it is firm.

If a spouse is suspected of cheating, or if there is estrangement in a marriage because someone is testing the ties of trust, or if parents and children experience crises of trust, these are most troubling — even traumatic — happenings. When custodians of our financial securities give us reason to feel insecure, we take notice and action. Such situations create vortices that suck up all the energies of a person, distracting her or him from the public zones. In addition, the recognition of trouble in the private or intimate spheres, because these relate in complex ways to the public, should lead to some sort of action. It is difficult to speak credibly about successfully building cultures of trust among those who never experience any of these in close-up cases where an individual could be expected to exercise some measure of control.

While the vividness and palpability of domestic and private trust issues are prime, the members of the public do not have the luxury of neglecting contexts of these. Thus a citizen who asks whether his investments are relatively safe or whether he will be a victim of swindles and scams because weak laws and casual enforcement do not protect him well will be agitated, sometimes too late, over issues that demand governmental supervision. Similarly, the ordinary citizen who is unequipped to judge whether certain pharmaceuticals are life-enhancing or dangerous can judge what officials to elect or what kinds of supervisory agencies a society should demand. If a graduate student loses place and thus employment opportunities because classmates cheat, she will be concerned with fairness. Will her university possess effective means of supervising examinations so that no one can easily cheat? A citizen has to trust public servants such as firefighters and police to live up to their responsibilities. All these instances are reminders that the public and the private spheres are webbed even in personal cases.

On the next level, in the decisively public sphere, certain kinds of issues make most insistent demands. The first one that comes to mind has to do with military and governmental affairs: both demand trust on the part of citizens and create trauma when trust breaks down. The second is the area of economic and commercial life, which depends on trust in areas where contracts and covenants cannot do all the work. The delivery and assurance of health care is another large aspect of experience that depends on trust. No doubt in a separate category — but just as vital — are trust issues among and between those represented by the words "science" and "religion," as these are transacted in public life. Bibliographies on "why the science and religion debates matter" are extensive.[1] Furthermore, they are growing because of the increasing tension among those who are devoted to science and religion and who have much at stake in issues generated and affected by both.

That which is centuries old is recognized in labels for eras, such as the "age of science" or the "age of technology." The forces, energies, and inventions in such ages are obvious to all. But the pole represented by "science" is not the only one that is making news and sharpening issues; "religion" is also ever more engrossing, promising, and threatening. The predictions of many visionaries in the eighteenth century, when the belief in progress received new impetus, centered on visions of the ways religious people were threatened and their downfall foreseen. However, millions of them did not oblige the prophets of scientific imperialism and hegemony by disappearing. While in much of Europe, it is true, the decline in the power of religious institutions and the measurements of positive religious interest have drastically declined, in most of the world the old religions have revived and become assertive. Often their rise has led many among

1. Typical of such literature is Fraser Watts and Kevin Dutton, *Why Science and Religion Dialogue Matters* (Philadelphia: Templeton, 2006).

them to challenge science and the institutions devoted to it. The challenge does not mean that the religious have cut themselves off from the fruits of scientific discovery. They enjoyed health-giving medical discoveries and the benefits of technology, quickened as it was by scientific research.

How Conflicts Developed

When advocates for scientific dominion and those for religious dominion displayed self-assurance, their spheres often collided. Many scientific and religious leaders became suspicious of each other, and they often broke trust. Most of the specific programs and activities among scientists, of course, are not designed to breed mistrust of religion. Experimenters and developers in the fields of science, be they personally religious or not, tend to go about their formal and focused business with indifference to religious faith and different faiths; they find them irrelevant to their immediate purposes. Some may show interest in the details of the particular religion of which they are at least casual — and possibly engaged — members; but the cognitive claims of theologians in general concern most of them less, because such claims seem to make little difference to their worlds and work. At the same time, on the other side many religious groups prosper. And among those groups, some leaders, pressing their faith-based claims, encourage mistrust of science. The publics associated with such leaders can be stirred to counter with aggressive defenses of religion as they understand it, or at least defenses of their own religion.

When a breakdown of trust and empathy has occurred in science, religion, or some other realm, a new and unwelcome character often appears on the scene in the form of the fanatic. "Mr. Dooley," a fictional creation of a Chicago journalist almost a century ago, described the role of such an extremist in religion and politics. The fanatic, Dooley said, knows that he is doing exactly what the Lord would be doing if the Lord were also in possession of the facts. Yet "facts" are mostly not at issue: what is at issue is the interpretation of the facts. In the microbiological and neuro-scientific fields, some experts do make claims that out of these they can develop an ethic to replace the moral patterns long associated with religion. In the religious world, similar fanatics make claims that scientific knowledge and know-how have been revealed to them in their sacred books. Dialogues between Dooleyites do not occur; shouting matches or snubbings do.

Enmity, Neglect, and Dialogue

People do not need to be overcome by frustration or to choose prideful isolation. They seek alternatives to such futilities. "There are three possible attitudes toward the relation between science and religion: enmity, neglect, and dialogue." So says Sjoerd L. Bonting at the beginning of *Creation and Double Chaos: Science and Theology in Discussion.*[2] We can conceive of more, but these will do for making the point. All three of them can contribute to a climate and culture of mistrust and suspicion.

First, *enmity* kills occasions for trusting, for in enmity one invents the other as stranger and then conceives of that invented other, the stranger, in negative, often-menacing, and always conversation-killing terms. At root in enmity is what philosopher Richard Rorty has called "philosophy envy" in his criticism of those scientists who argue that ethics develops through the interaction of neuron firings in the brain.[3]

The second attitude, *neglect,* may not contribute to a culture of distrust simply because leaders on both sides find the other uninteresting and irrelevant to the personal search of society's need. Instead, trust, nontrust, distrust, and mistrust do not come into play in this case because partisans conceive of the other as inconsequential or even totally irrelevant.

I have spoken in this book of *dialogue,* the third attitude or practice observed by Bonting, as a potential instrument for cultivating trust. This does not mean that an individual who enters dialogue can simply extend trust to the partners in conversation. To use Oakeshott's term, conversation could "descend" into argument of a sort that would leave issues unresolved, individuals silenced or even defeated, and citizens finally exiled from the zones where participation can occur. A potential participant in such an encounter would feel threatened and would fear that her vulnerabilities would be exposed and the risks of loss might be too high. Still, more positive experiences can occur if those who sponsor or encourage dialogue properly set the stage.

2. Sjoerd L. Bonting, *Creation and Double Chaos: Science and Theology in Discussion* (Minneapolis: Fortress, 2005), p. 1.
3. Richard Rorty, "Philosophy Envy," *Daedalus* (Fall 2004): 22.

What Good Is Conversation?

So, the stage is set. Concern for dialogue or conversation is accompanied by practical questions, such as, What good is it? and What is to accompany or follow it? Such concerns should crowd the mind of any who carefully read definitions of conversation. I have pointed to some of them in the writings of philosopher Michael Oakeshott and theologian David Tracy. For Oakeshott, we recall once more, the "components of culture" can be thought of as "voices, each the expression of a distinct and conditional understanding, and of the culture itself as these voices joined, as such voices could only be joined, in a conversation — an endless unrehearsed intellectual adventure in which, in imagination, we enter into a variety of modes of understanding the world and ourselves...."[4] "'Endless?!' Stop already!" we can imagine someone saying: "We are busy people and have many concerns on our minds, including many that are associated with science, religion, and public life. What is the point of 'endless' ventures? It's time to talk about possible practical outcomes."

Similarly, we can picture someone who seeks to replace mistrust with trust growing impatient while Tracy describes conversation as a "game where we learn to give in to the movement required by questions worth exploring."[5] "A 'game'? Stop!" We can now imagine another someone saying, "Get serious. The issues are too portentous for us to play around with them, or to leave us content with questions — never answers — which, as Tracy insists, 'must control every conversation.'" "When," the citizen legitimately asks, "do we get some answers?" Perhaps the partners in conversation could find refuge in argument. Yet, it is with science and religion as it is with history: the task of his fellow historians, historian Pieter Geyl famously said, is to prosecute "an argument without end."

Whoever takes seriously the complexities of science, religion, and politics knows that, while argument may settle certain kinds of issues, conversation is not assumed to be such a settling entity. It would be strange for anyone to claim, "I surely won that conversation today."

4. Timothy Fuller, ed., *The Voice of Liberal Learning: Michael Oakeshott on Education* (New Haven, CT: Yale University Press, 1989), pp. 38-39.
5. David Tracy, *Plurality and Ambiguity* (San Francisco: Harper and Row, 1987), pp. 18-19.

Conversation is, as Oakeshott says, "unrehearsed" and adventurous, though, one hopes, not uninformed. Such discourse reveals its intrinsic value for the role it plays in keeping people informed as they go about their inquiries. They are encouraged to listen, without turning triumphant as they might if conclusions were the goals.

With so much at stake, and since there is rich promise in conversation and what it implies, it is important to develop an understanding of this form of human exchange as an agency for constructing cultures of trust. To inform that discussion, I return once more to Oakeshott, whose war against "category mistakes" could be misinterpreted by some as a move toward a dead end, an end that would best be defined as compartmentalization, which would be the death of dialogue. In compartmentalization the concerns of "science" would fit in one figurative slot in the brain, "religion" in another, and "politics" in a third. Each would represent a deposit to be defended by specialists, not agents of potential human understanding. Oakeshott himself may have regarded his own expression to be an invitation to such a judgment. Thus, in some minds, "modes" equal "compartments." In later writings, without abandoning the distinctive contribution of modal definition, Oakeshott helpfully adds the metaphor of "voices."

His revised definition comes in an essay in which he reveals his mistrust of those who "assure us that all human utterance is in one mode." True, they recognize "a certain variety of utterance, but they hear only one authentic voice." He reviews once more some "other modes of speaking, the voice of practical activity, the voices of 'poetry' and of 'science,' and 'history.'" Then comes the polemic: the kind of monopolistic understanding he has just described, "while appearing to accommodate a variety of voices, in fact recognizes only one, namely, the voice of argumentative discourse, the voice of 'science', and all others are acknowledged merely in respect of their aptitude to imitate this voice." He follows this with a decisive turn: "Yet, it may be supposed that the diverse idioms of utterance which make up current human intercourse have some meeting-place and compose a manifold of some sort. And, as I understand it, the image of this meeting-place is not an inquiry or an argument, but a conversation."[6]

6. Michael Oakeshott, "The Voice of Poetry in the Conversation of Mankind," in *Rationalism in Politics and Other Essays* (Indianapolis: Liberty Press, 1962), p. 489.

Conversation as a Meeting Place and a Manifold

I had to look up the noun "manifold" in this context; I knew about the manifold as part of an automobile, but I found it also defined as "a whole that unites or consists of many diverse elements," and thus does it match the idea of a "meeting-place." A conversation takes the form of both the distribution of ideas and their convergence, their meeting. Conversation, Oakeshott agrees, may be inconclusive, unending, playful, a game, but it is also a potential contributor to human good that complements and supplements the ways argument can advance that good. This "appropriate image of human intercourse — appropriate because it recognizes the qualities, the diversities, and the proper relationships of human utterances" — thus offers a "manifold" or place of "meeting." In the matter of science and religion (or when it is argued about as "science versus religion") Oakeshott allows for the obvious: "Of course there is argument and inquiry and information, but wherever these are profitable they are to be recognized as passages in this conversation, and perhaps they are not the most captivating of the passages."

We note that Oakeshott, taking a moment to let his wit show, writes that "the ability to participate in this conversation . . . distinguishes the human being from the animal and the civilized man from the barbarian. Indeed, it seems not improbable that it was the engagement in this conversation . . . that gave us our present appearance, man being descended from a race of apes who sat in talk so long and so late that they wore out their tails." This kind of talk, "in the end," gives place and character "to every human activity and utterance." And it was "in the end" because, of course, the immediate field of moral activity is the world of practical enterprise. An intellectual achievement appears, in the first place, within each of the various universes of discourse. Therefore, scientists who want to help heal and shelter people must first tend to their homework as specialists, engaging in experimental projects and the imparting of information. Then they might converse — or at least try to. Again, "in the end," Oakeshott says, "this conversation is not only the greatest but also the most hardly sustained of all the accomplishments of mankind."[7]

Whereas "category mistakes" threaten the modes of discourse, pride also endangers the voices of conversation. "For each voice," says Oakeshott, "is prone to *superbia,* that is, an exclusive concern with its

---

7. Oakeshott, "The Voice of Poetry," pp. 489-91.

own utterance. . . ." Whenever we hear a bloviating cleric dismissing both science and the scientist, or an arrogant scientist dismissing out of hand all that religion and the religions have represented and do represent, we have a right to be impatient or petulant, because such *superbia* tends to return to barbarism. Where monologue or monopoly by one voice would take over a conversation, Oakeshott asks for more kinds of voices, for example, "to consider again the voice of poetry, to consider it as it speaks in the conversation." Poetry, for him, stood for all the creative arts, in which one views the human scene *sub specie imaginationis.* To be sure the reader gets the point, the philosopher strings together some verb forms about "the self making and recognizing images," thus, "sensing, perceiving, feeling, desiring, thinking, believing, contemplating, supposing, knowing, preferring, approving, laughing, crying, dancing, loving, singing, making hay, devising mathematical demonstrations" — as each has its place as an "identifiable mode of imagining."[8]

Arguments posed as ballistics in the "warfare between science and theology" or "religion versus science" might have or might have had their place in the political order (where the *polis* refers to communal life within government, the academy, the clinics, or commerce). The voice of science, represented by some scientists, when given to *superbia* and when claiming privilege or a monopoly as arbiter of the true, the good, and the beautiful, may abandon all conversation and take on only the character of argument. At that point the voices of history, poetry, or "practice" are tempted to argue back. The efforts toward conversation would be futile, since true communication is by then impossible. If the voice of practice, as it comes from authoritarian politicians or religious exclusivists, disrupts inquiry or conversation, the voices of science, history, and poetry may in the short range engage in argument, but one cannot expect much communication.

By the very nature of the case, the arguments cannot well serve the "manifold" interests. Certainly, there can be criticisms — for example, when a religious group oversteps lines of distinction between religion and the civil authority (in line with "separation of church and state," variously defined and defended). Those who disagree with a proposition have a right and duty to argue against them. On the basics and at root, however, the diverse voices will be ineffective if they engage in making category mistakes.

8. Oakeshott, "The Voice of Poetry," p. 496.

Sjoerd Bonting, who brought up the subjects of "enmity, neglect, and dialogue," occasioning our return to the theme of conversation, did his own elaborating. Thus scientists and theologians, he says, in our time express enmity "as the result of misconceptions about the tenets and limitations of the two disciplines." As examples, he cites some fundamentalist literalists' offering their narrowed vision of religion and scientists given to scientism (in which they "maintain that science can explain all aspects of life") as equally confusing categories or drowning out other voices. Neglect, he claims, was evident typically in the designation by Stephen J. Gould of science and religion as two "non-overlapping magisteria." Similarly, Belgian philosopher Mia Gosselin concludes that the two disciplines will be "eternally irreconcilable" unless Christians try to reconcile by simply watering down their faith to the point of its becoming meaningless.[9]

Offering an alternative, I will illustrate the point with the distinctively Christian voice of Sjoerd Bonting, who speaks with favor and hope of a new situation in which notable writers have effectively bridged worlds and worldviews, writers such as Ian Barbour, Arthur Peacocke, and John Polkinghorne. Any number of other theological participants might be cited as having offered parallel proposals. To bring issues forward, as a sample, Bonting includes in his purposes a critique of the concept of *creatio ex nihilo* ("creation out of nothing"), which he challenges with the vision of "creation and the double chaos." Lest defensive believers see this critique as counter to biblical teaching, he reminds readers that *ex nihilo* is not the teaching of the biblical book of Genesis. Drawing on the thinkers just mentioned, Bonting offers six summary suggestions, and I find them to be quite accurate conclusions to draw after considerable reading on the subject. To advance them, he introduces the word "worldview," which could be translated more modestly in our context as the language of "modes" and "voices." It will be most efficient simply to reproduce here his statements on science and theology, the latter of which we shall treat as part of the genus *religion*. Readers should regard his remarks as more typical than definitive:

1. Science and theology provide two worldviews of a single reality, the cosmos in which we live. Both are God-given in the sense that God is revealed through human minds and hands not only in Scripture,

9. Bonting, *Creation and Double Chaos*, pp. 1-2.

but also in the scientific insight that God allowed us to develop through our senses and brainpower.

2. Both worldviews have limitations. Science cannot deal with the "beyond." It can tell us about mechanisms but not about purpose; it can answer *how* questions. Theology cannot properly deal with the scientific aspects of this world. It can tell us about purpose but little about mechanisms; it can answer *why* questions.

3. A dialogue between the two worldviews is possible, because the two disciplines have much in common. Both seek a rational explanation of basic data: biblical data in the case of theology and observational and experimental data in the case of science. Both have certain axioms in common, such as "Nothing can both be and not be at the same time and in the same respect."

4. Dialogue is needed in order to achieve a deeper understanding of the world in which we live and, hopefully, to solve some of the problems posed by it (for instance, bioethical problems).

5. Dialogue requires that each discipline be taken in its integrity. The two disciplines may challenge each other on a particular point, such as the virgin birth. However, it is not permissible to reject a well-founded theory like the evolution theory in order to uphold a literal interpretation of the six days of creation in Genesis 1.

6. The meeting ground for the two disciplines is to be found primarily in creation theology on the one side and cosmic and biological evolution on the other side.[10]

My reservation would be to contest his statement number 3, especially the part about the theologian seeking a "rational explanation of . . . biblical data." Some may do so, but theirs is not the whole story. Rationality and reason, one may insist, need not be alien to religious inquiry and discourse, but the concept of seeing them as chief responses to "biblical data" seems confining. Still, Bonting's proposition can be translated to other terms, and his counsel in general still provides a framework.

Leaving Bonting's particular approach aside, a scholar — after asking what has come of the conversation to date — may observe it in action and may make some assessments about future programs. That the conversation has begun or has been renewed in fresh forms is obvious.

---

10. Bonting, *Creation and Double Chaos*, pp. 2-3.

On numerous college and university campuses, and at professional conferences, a growing cohort of scientists and religionists have pioneered in this mode of conversation, understanding as their conversation develops how limiting and even futile it is to be measured by one universe of discourse, one mode of experience, the monopolizing sound of one voice among all the others.

An example among many with which I am familiar has been the impetus given interdisciplinary conversation by the Templeton Foundation, which has venturesomely sponsored individuals and groups, notably in academic settings, to engage in the conversations I have been describing. As a sometime and relatively marginal participant, I have observed scholars who have come to new understandings in their efforts to promote the human good. Of course, mistakes and false starts are common in such endeavors. On occasion I have been uneasy when some researchers would make tentative theological claims based on measurement. For instance, at one Templeton conference session, pictures of human brain activity were shown via "power point," their blues and yellows and greens looking familiar, as they appear in many such SCAN pictures. They revealed different forms of brain activities depending on whether the pictured brain belonged to someone who was doing "Buddhist" or "Christian" meditating. One challenger to claims based on such measurements and imaging countered them by reminding us that nothing specifically religious or theological — and even nothing that could be translated into such spheres — had been shown. One could find such differences, he reminded us, in displayed records of brain activity from the brain owner's responses to aesthetic or sensual, not necessarily religious, delights.

Now and then the question "How large is God?" would be posed in the company of scientists, as it was once in a book-length forum — with two humanists thrown in for good measure. (I was one of the humanists, my branch of the humanities being history of religion.) Here again, the editors and some authors were using the scientific mode, which sees things *sub specie quantitatis,* and they were making what appeared to me to be a categorical mistake by then transferring the inquiry and findings to the other modes, such as history, poetry, or "the practical." I have no doubt that scientists similarly faulted the religionists when the latter, in turn, used the vocabulary and concerns distinctive to the practical mode. Still, the published symposia volumes did not come apart at the spine. The oral presentations in the symposium proceeded with no great physical danger to participants who brought diverse universes of discourse into play.

The Templeton scholarships, conferences, and individual projects have demonstrated that world-class scientists, especially in disciplines relating to medical research, cosmology, evolution, and brain research, can participate and make contributions to religious inquiry and discourse. Some critics from the scientific communities offer the opinion that the scientists who engage in conversation with theological ethicists have to be betraying, a priori, their medical commitments to science. Instead, those criticized scientists were joining in the conversation of which Oakeshott had spoken, and they were doing so without losing the integrity of their disciplines. All the while they were opening themselves to the need to revise their professional goals. They were probing what is distinctively human without suggesting that syntheses had to emerge, or suggesting that some truth halfway between the sciences in question and religious modes and voices was necessary — or even salutary.

A Templeton Foundation brochure quotes some notables who reinforce the theme we find illuminated by Oakeshott's delineation of modes.[11] Thus Oxford biochemist and theologian Arthur Peacocke writes in terms that could parallel Oakeshott's theme that "experience is a whole," but it is grasped through "arrests in human experiences," the modes or voices. He says: "The universe has one reality. Science and religion are ultimately converging in that the scientific and theological enterprises are two interacting and mutually reinforcing approaches to reality. Both fields are alive with ever-changing ideas. The great physicists — Newton, Maxwell, Einstein — knew this, and were more judicious and humble than many of today's scientists about answers science can really deliver." Another of many possibilities appears in this witness from Nobel Prize–winner Charles Townes: "Science wants to know the mechanism of the universe, religion the meaning. The two cannot be separated. Many scientists feel there is no place in research for discussion of anything that sounds mystical. But it is unreasonable to think we already know enough about the natural world to be confident about the totality of forces." Such a summary could only grow out of the experience of a scientist who long has participated in the science-

---

11. The quotations are strewn along the way in the brochure entitled *John Templeton Foundation* (Radnor, PA: Templeton, 2001).

and-religion conversations, who has listened well, has much to say, and gets a hearing.

A still further distillation of the experience of conversation comes from Francis Collins, who directed the Human Genome Project, the most ambitious endeavor of its kind under United States Government auspices. In 2009 he was appointed to head the National Institutes of Health. More explicit about his Christian faith in a personal God than are many scientists in the sustained conversation, Collins has seen his faith as complementing his approach to science and its "facts," just as he pursues his scientific efforts in the light of faith. His personal witness has mystified some scientists who are non- or antireligious; but they have not found a basis in this context for criticizing his science, even as he sees positive societal roles for faith.

> As we see science in genetics, medicine, and biology advancing at a prodigious rate, we also see stronger reasons than ever to determine how this relates to matters of the spirit. . . . My own personal perspective as a scientist who won't accept facts without having rigorous data is that I am still entirely comfortable having a relationship with a personal God who is not bounded by science the way I am. There is no discordance between being a rigorous scientist who demands data to answer natural questions and being a person of faith whose God responds to personal prayer. Science is a great way to explore the natural, but a lousy way to explore the supernatural.

Standing at such a juncture when panelists for conferences are being invited allows for an observation about suspicions and prejudices that may well stunt or limit knowledge that could be of use to all kinds and conditions of people. Such was evident to me when a national academy sought my nominations for panelists who could represent science on one hand and religious thought on the other. Some scientists on the panel, though they were open to such a conference program, balked when the names of certain accomplished physician-ethicists were brought forward. Some were offended when they learned that this or that scientist professed faith in a personal God. But none of them could demonstrate that such a belief compromised the scientific endeavors in which such a scientist was involved.

Battles over evolution in each generation bring forth the most publicized controversy. Issues in neuroscience promise to pose the most exciting new issues for scientists and religious thinkers who are open to the conversation. However, more creative dialogue goes on with respect to the way science and religion relate to illness, health, and medicine than in other spheres. Here I can add another reference from personal experience. During a twenty-year period ending in 1998, I was assigned to be a founding president and then senior scholar of the Park Ridge Center for the Study of Health, Faith, and Ethics in Chicago under the auspices of the Advocate Health Care System. The arrival of Laurence O'Connell as director brought expertise in medical ethics. I was to bring my historian's interest in these questions to the table, defined, in Oakeshott's terms, as my "mode of experience," to see these matters *sub specie praeteritorum,* which means with the past not only in view but even dominant in research questions and proposals.

In the course of the years at the Park Ridge Center we produced a full shelf of volumes on faith traditions and how they dealt with health and medicine. Each of these volumes came out of an antecedent symposium in which people from each of the faith traditions participated — to represent a viewpoint, to criticize it, and to hear others. While we historians might enjoy enclave existence with those who share our "voice in the conversation," our "mode" or "arrest in experience," anyone familiar with concerns about the body, health, and illness had to realize that we knew that history is a relatively minor, though still essential, partner to this inquiry. We needed and did include at the table some scientists, some poets (yes, poets!), and medical practitioners at every turn.

Around the conference table and in the clinics, we participants had virtually daily opportunities to see and experience the trust shown by people of one school of thought to others, from one discipline to other disciplines, and, if they were active in a faith community, how the two worlds described by Francis Collins came together. The Park Ridge Center attracted scientific leaders from around the world and from the major world religions. They greatly broadened and deepened the inquiries, just as they complicated the thought of those who were protecting sectarian or single-disciplinary turf. Year by year we saw the enclave mentality challenged and eroded, and we were cheered to see that it was seldom accompanied or replaced by the dread phenomena of philosophical syncretism, theological imperialism, or simple relativism. That is to say, participants grew in their trust of the "other voices." They learned from each other ways that argument by itself could not have fostered. Highly informed people who brought strong opinions voiced them freely and made clear that they were learning from each other. No one was ever silenced, insulted, or goaded into exile.

So constant and consistent were the results of this conversational process that the Park Ridge Center, prompted and supported by the Pew Charitable Trusts, was asked to produce what became *Religion and Public Discourse: Principles and Guidelines for Religious Participants.*[12] Participants included representatives of Islam, Native American traditions, Baha'i, Reform Judaism, Buddhism, Orthodox Judaism, Hinduism, and a dozen varieties of Christianity. All of them had participated in conversations with philosophers, but this was an attempt for religious voices to find coherence in their approaches and to build trust among each other — something that may be harder for religionists to do than it is for scientists.

Here is the brief sample of a "How to . . ." of contributing to the building of cultures — or at least elements of subcultures — of trust. It comes in the form of "Guidelines for Structuring Public Policy Discourse Involving Diverse People of Faith." Throughout this book I have discussed mistrust based on miscommunication or noncommunication, not only between scientists and religionists but also among people in both camps. For "science" versus "religion," one simply mixes in the complicating factor that we have associated with the diverse "modes of experience" and "voices."

This counsel helps set the stage in terms with which we are working: "Create an atmosphere conducive to the cultivation of trust." In the general text of this document, page one comes to the point at once: "When people of religious faith enter public debate, they draw on their deepest beliefs — and sometimes express themselves with a passion and vehemence that can quickly turn conversation into argument, and argument into rhetorical meltdown." That kind of observation was based on, among other events, the 1994 Cairo International Conference on Population and Development. There "believers made their presence felt on all sides in a stunning encounter . . . [when] people of conviction shocked each other and a watching world as they clashed over some of the most volatile topics of the day," most of them related to sexual and biological issues. Many of them regularly related to scientists in joint address to such topics. The Park Ridge Center participants

12. Published by the Park Ridge Center, Chicago, Illinois, in 1998.

were convinced that there were better ways — than those convention-ally used — to represent faiths and display convictions.

The *Religion and Public Discourse* document is out of print, and until it appears online we will have to be content with some summary statements. "Those who participate in discourse in the public square . . .

1. welcome the diversity of beliefs and opinions;
2. recognize civil discourse as a process;
3. realize and teach that profound social issues have religious dimensions;
4. understand that religious belief frequently calls for some form of civil discourse."

As for "Covenants of Conversation, those who participate . . .

1. pledge to act and speak with integrity and to regard others as doing so;
2. articulately express their faith;
3. act respectfully in the face of nonreligious knowledge because of religious limits;
4. speak to failures and mistakes of [their] co-believers."

Third, with respect to "Engaging the Other, those who participate. . .

1. make efforts to engage on a personal level;
2. tell stories;
3. act on the basis of relative and partial agreements;
4. listen to the voices of those previously excluded;
5. put words into action."

Finally, there was comment on "Living with Conflict" during and after conversation and argument, when "those who participate . . .

1. recognize that conflict is inevitable and can be creative;
2. take steps to assure that the conversation moves beyond conflict or stalemate;
3. inventory the religious resources and bring them forth."

The document closes with a statement on "The Hope of Civil Discourse" in terms that can apply when people with scientific and religious interests come together, even if this document only assumes the place of science as it is directed to religious participants:

> All life is meeting. That is the starting point for discovery, the prompter of conversation, the understanding that promotes change among humans. People of profound commitment who feared that meeting the "other" face to face might lead them to lose their convictions, instead have found a deepening of their own faith and philosophy. By hearing the other, they also grow, and this growth includes the readiness to pursue the common good in imaginative ways. In the end, as in the beginning, conversation among people who disagree is the most promising approach when people address the troubling yet potentially creative issues of our time.

Yes, in such programs there has been some rhetorical softening of positions and some adaptations, as one hopes would appear in any dynamic scientific or religious tradition. Revisiting the most dramatic science-religion controversy is helpful here: the dialogue between evolutionary scientists and (especially) Christian theologians since 1859, the year of the publication of Darwin's *The Origin of Species*. There was massive resistance to anything having to do with evolution when the book appeared. Historians of science have had their fun with the early theological responses, in which, in retrospect, the Christian leaders did make fools of themselves. (Those leaders might counter that many of the scientists did as well.) From the first, however, some theologians kept the conversation going and came up with other promising viewpoints. Back when Lamarckian evolution had been dominant, it was easy for some theologians to say that "evolution is God's way of doing things," because in such a reading, purpose and design still ruled. Such a bridging was more difficult when "chance" came to characterize talk about evolutionary processes. It was more difficult, if not impossible, to "fit" God into a scheme that seemed so random, chaotic, and purposeless.

As scientists and theologians through a century recognized that coming to some understanding was urgent in their separate communities and for the national good, they grew more inventive. Today, official Roman Catholicism has withdrawn most of its earlier condemnations of evolution and endorsed evolutionary inquiry, while still working to assure a witness to some integral theological themes. The same tends to be the case in a number of brands of Judaism and in mainline Protestantism. In general, conservative Protestantism has held the line, and where it does not simply react against and resist evolutionary research and exposition, it has come up with very minor concessions to them.

As I have mentioned, any adaptation has been treated with scorn by people we might call "scientific fundamentalists," that is, non- or anti-religious evolutionists who have a dated view of the dynamics of theological thought. They claim that every adaptation within a faith community represents the kind of compromising that is easy to deride. Meanwhile, Christian theological thought, independent of any conversations with evolutionary scientists who practice a faith, turned defensive or even aggressive, based on the dynamics of the occasion. In the mid-twentieth century it emerged in such inventions as "creation research," a category mistake that led to confusion and the distorting of diverse "modes" and the stifling of other "voices."

In political controversy, where trust had broken down, creation research came to be deemed formally religious and therefore not to be permitted as an option or a preference in public schools. So some critics of evolution came up with "intelligent design" as an explanation of human origins and development. Like the creation research people and their cause, the supporters of intelligent design tried to bring to the table at school board meetings a sophisticated approach over against evolutionary science. We must mention this only briefly as part of a status report, since fair treatment of "the warfare between science and theology" — or the conversation of scientists and religionists — would demand and has already produced a vast literature that carries beyond the point of illustration I am trying to make.

The dialogue with scientists has led biblical scholars to rely more on the poetic mysteries of Job 38-42 rather than Genesis 1-3, meaning that they have wanted to put a stop to the category mistake of treating and using a religious text as a scientific text, such use being alien to its nature. It has also led notable scientific scholars to be more ready to acknowledge the distinct "other" voice of religion as having an integrity of its own. As scientists and religious thinkers turn from suspicion and hostility to visions of complementarity, they have provided a richer repertory of options for people who struggle "doing" science while "making sense" of religious meanings.

Leaving the issue at this point causes me to return to some of the language I used earlier about human limits and limitations in their inventions. I have used no verbal sleight of hand to suggest that the conversation we have been discussing settles or brings to conclusion the points at issue. The dialogue does not produce satisfying proofs for the existence of God or the truth about non-God — a-theism. It does not promise to resolve all points of controversy, something that by definition could not be done given the immensity of the issues and the complexity of methods and approaches. Having trust in each other might bring people to the table and elevate the discourse there, but trust does not lead to agreement where agreement would be difficult if not impossible to achieve. Yet the results of trust-making ventures in these fields pay off in the creation of a climate in which scientists and religionists both are able to pursue inquiries with humane and humanistic purposes, without having to apologize or defend themselves, thus distracting them from their more important work, which is to advance scientific and religious discovery and to enlarge on their points of tentative agreement. The implications for political life are obvious, since the political order includes all the people who bring to the table such wide ranges of opinion and belief in science and religion.

Holmes Rolston III, an accomplished participant in the conversations among scientists and theologians or other religious thinkers, has published seven books on these subjects. But here I will quote what he says in a brief contribution to a symposium about why the dialogue between science and religion matters. As with my condensation of the Park Ridge Center statement, I will here reproduce Rolston's thesis statements without fleshing them out or quoting the details of what he has written. My purpose is to provide prompts for debate and conversation, and it is profitable to toss these statements out in mixed company and go on from there.

Here are six reasons why the dialogue is vital:

1. Science cannot teach us what we need most to know about nature — that is, how to value it.
2. Science cannot teach us what we most need to know about culture — that is, how to value it.
3. Science increasingly opens up religious questions.
4. The future of religion depends on the dialogue.
5. Dialogue offers new opportunities for understanding and confronting suffering and evil.

6. The dialogue between science and religion matters because the future of Earth depends on it.[13]

Only the naïve, untutored, or illiterate could picture any of these as being acceptable theses for conversation or argument among the fundamentalist "new atheists" or fundamentalist Christians. Neither one trusts the other or trusts anyone who would bring them to the table to converse. As for argument, both sets of absolutist partisans contend that the debate is over and that there are no shared premises for debate because there is nothing to converse about. One would not start the trust-building process with people at these extremes, though it would not be appropriate to rule them out of all future consideration. Meanwhile, there are enough people who thrive between those two categories and who are open to the dialogue, for reasons suggested by Rolston.

Inconclusive Conclusion: Continuing Conversation

This book began with an imagined conversation among readers and this author. It comes to an end not with a conclusion, but with a continuing conversation. Michael Oakeshott, David Tracy, and other theorists speak of conversation as unrehearsed, open-ended, capable of producing positive yields, but never ended the way arguments end. Picture the skeptical conversationalists returning after 200 pages with something like this:

"So, author, do you *really* think that developing and proliferating cultures of trust can make a contribution to human good in the face of the well-advertised crises of trust, whose existence you obviously recognize?"

"Yes."

"Let's take a reality check," the skeptic comes back. "Can you agree with me that 'the powers,' namely governments, mass media of communication, commerce and markets, political parties, institutions of education, lawyers and judges, partisans in wars, medical establishments, and even religious institutions, are experiencing profound problems with trust. We hear and read about almost cosmic levels of

---

13. Holmes Rolston III, "The Science and Religion Dialogue: Why It Matters," in Watts and Dutton, eds., *Why Science and Religion Dialogue Matters*, pp. 33-37.

mistrust, distrust, lack of trustworthiness, broken trust, and you agree that they exist. I want to be sure I am reading you right."

"You are reading me right, though chronicling these problems has not been the main burden of these chapters. They receive plenty of attention every day in public media and conversation on the street, so we have taken them for granted, and we've moved on to other ways of addressing the problems."

"Reality check number two," the conversation partner continues — in what seems to be coming closer to an argument than a dialogue. "And you suggest that it makes a difference if citizens put energies into inventing, developing, and encouraging what you call 'cultures of trust'? You think it is important to make urgent the task of devoting those energies of persons in families, intimate partnerships, neighborhoods, schools, congregations, workplaces, precincts, voluntary organizations, and more — to building and enjoying cultures of trust?"

"Yes, you heard me right," I respond, "and I hope you are at least partially convinced — convinced enough to continue the conversation. I count eight or more 'zones' in that one sentence. I'd want to think more about strategies in each case, but for now, yes, this agenda signals what is important."

"Still more," you say. "And you picture that such cultures can influence the less intimate zones of life, the 'higher-up' establishments of power, the great systems of management and control? Isn't that a utopian dream?"

"It could be seen as utopian if you picture me imagining that there is some enormous magic pill that will solve problems connected with trust. It is also utopian if you think that all this depends on sunny views of human nature, assumptions that people are naturally trusting and trustworthy. Just the opposite: because the human drama, the history of cultures and societies, shows more examples of trust broken than trust kept, more of human weakness than of natural human strength, it is important to work out strategies that will bring some improvements. I have called this approach 'meliorative' with an 'incremental' vision."

"You sound as though you are scaling back your expectations," you say, ". . . and mine — if I brought hopes for a 'cure' for our problems. I'm back to beginnings. What difference does this all make?"

"This is not a simple 'trickle-up' approach," I explain, "that suggests that if we do well on intimate, local, interpersonal, small-scale ventures, the benefits of trust will seep up. But I have pictured some symbiosis among the cultures of trust, some interpenetration of the zones their builders inhabit, some contagion. This occurs because of example, precedent, and the enjoyment of the efficiency that trust-relations can generate."

"Such as . . . ?" you ask.

"Picture 'trust' as an intrinsic good. Like 'the virtues,' it has positive value by its very existence. Imagine the extrinsic values. If children in elementary school are participants in an environment where teachers are trustworthy and capable of generating trust among students, they will have examples and precedents — and habits! — that they can carry over to college classrooms and their communications over the Internet, which currently is an instrument for breakers of trust. Think of the Internet scams. Think of the swindles. Think of the positives that occur when people communicate honestly.

"Picture a company in which top management has been shown to be trustworthy and has taken pains to create subcultures in which breaking trust is something that 'simply isn't done around here.' Picture a complex organization in which people on all levels learn to trust each other and do not have to put all their efforts into monitoring each other. Isn't working in such a place an obvious benefit, one that rubs off on the families of workers, on clients, and on customers?

"Picture parishes and congregations, where restoration of trust is so difficult after clerical abuse or financial scandal, enjoying restored trust and bringing new expectations to clergy, hierarchs, and staffs. Picture legislatures in which a significant number of lawmakers through the years conscientiously serve publics through the ways they exemplify trustworthiness."

"Enough!" you say. "I still think you are overdoing the long case study that is at the heart of this book. You invest so much in communication among those who live in distinct 'universes of discourse.' You suggest that if people in various professions, disciplines, and establishments could better understand where those in others are 'coming from,' and what differentiates the worlds of science, history, poetry, religion, and who knows what else, we would be better off."

"Indeed," say I.

"Back again to basics," you say. "If they understand the others' 'modes of experience' and their 'voices in conversation,' where will the conversation end? Will scientists who are not now at home in a religious universe of discourse going to be convinced, even converted, content that 'the existence of God' has been rationally proved and the positive values of religion recognized and assured? And will the people you call 'religionists,' if they are disdained, snubbed, overlooked, or excluded by scientists, be convinced by offerings of science that exclude religious phenomena and be happy with scientific reduction — in which religion is 'nothing but' this or that? And will their conversation improve public life?"

"What is the alternative to making these efforts?" I say in my (almost) final rhetorical question. "Are we better off when they are isolated from each other, hostile to each other, indifferent to one another — about some of the most profound and penetrating expressions of human endeavor? Are the paths of cynicism, arrogance, exclusion, or apathy better than trying to build cultures of trust? If mistrust closes off communication before it starts, and if distrust aborts understanding before the first words are spoken, it is impossible to pursue items further down the agenda. No, overcoming category mistakes, 'the most fatal of all errors,' will not produce final answers or utopia. Doing so, however, opens or continues a conversation that enhances cultures of trust. They strike me as not bad places to live."

"You said earlier," you respond, "that no one says, 'I sure won that conversation,' so I don't have to say that you 'won' anything. For now, let's simply agree to keep the conversation going."

"I am satisfied," say I, "if you got something of my point. I certainly heard your questionings. Can we consider our endeavors to favor 'incremental' and 'meliorative' steps, since we cannot produce utopia? The crisis of trust continues, but people in many disciplines and vocations are finding some creative ways to address it. They go about building subcultures and cultures of trust."

The motives of those builders will be varied. In the summer of 2009, an interviewer on National Public Radio talked with a physician who, on the larger scale, was trying to inspire trust in the reform of an ailing national health care system. On the more intimate scene, he was also treating patients who could not get health insurance and had no means of paying for emergency health care. I had been listening only casually to that radio conversation, but I became alert to the interviewer's last question, whose answer began to fade away, to be silenced in a moment. "Why do you do these two kinds of things?" she asked. *"Because I am a citizen,"* he replied. That was enough. Others might answer: "Because I am a believer," or "Because we share a common humanity, and the patients have needs." Hearing such responses would prompt any alert person to say, "And I trust you! Let's work to produce trustworthy systems." So they set about doing so in a time of desperate need.

Index